The Royal Parchment Scroll of Black Supremacy

Fitz Balintine Pettersburg

The Royal Parchment Scroll of Black Supremacy

W. Gabriel Selassie I

Orunmilla, Incorporated

Forward ©2017 W. Gabriel Selassie I
Preface © 2017 W. Gabriel Selassie I
Introduction © 2017 W. Gabriel Selassie I
Exegesis © 2017 W. Gabriel Selassie I

Orunmilla, Incorporated
106.5 Judge John Aiso St. #257
Los Angeles, California, USA
First Print 2017

All rights reserved. No part of this publication may be reproduced, stored in a retrieved system, or transmitted in any form or by any means electronic, mechanical, photocopying, or otherwise without the prior permission of Orunmilla, Incorporated.

Printed in the United States of America

Library of Congress Catalog Number: 2017919242

ISBN: ISBN: 978-0-9863819-2-8

Cover and Interior Design: Ghislain Viau

For
The Black Survivors

Contents

Forward	1
Preface	3
Introduction	5
A Guide to the Material	17
The Royal Parchment Scroll of Black Supremacy	19
Biblical Interpretation	133

Forward

It is my sincere desire to strike a blow at those conservative hearts that assert the only meaningful religious, and spiritual experiences are to be found in the mountains and valleys in of some far off land, some two thousand years ago, by people living in circumstances completely different than our own. The Royal Parchment Scroll of Black Supremacy is a revered and prophetic vision of the Ethiopian Kingdom's vault onto the modern world stage. Without a doubt Ethiopianism, the theological foundation for the Royal Parchment Scroll of Black Supremacy still has the power to move Black people. Simply witness the global Rastafari movement as it continues to engulf the Black Diaspora. The Royal Parchment Scroll of Black Supremacy is a haunting echo of people taken from Africa, sold into European chattel slavery and upon freedom, relegated to toil in a state of quasi-serfdom. The Royal Parchment Scroll of Black Supremacy is a triumph of the human spirit.

Jah Rastafari!
W. Gabriel Selassie I, Ph.D.

Preface

The purpose of this book is to provide a biblical exegesis of Royal Parchment Scroll of Black Supremacy (RPS). It would be easy to dismiss the RPS as evidence of a madman penning indecipherable gibberish. On the other hand, the RPS should be evaluated as valuable primary source theological document of Black Diasporic religious history that appropriately reflects the outcomes of centuries of slavery, segregation, apartheid, and colonialism. The RPS is an example of religious mythology. A religious mythology created by men and women who took it upon themselves to elevate their race to the status of Kings and Queens. The RPS was intended to awaken an inner spirit of the Black race by instilling race pride and rejecting a White interpretation of Christianity in favor of a Black interpretation. Fitz Balintine Pettersburg is due no less or no more praise as any of the authors who crafted the writings of the Abrahamic faiths or those responsible for disseminating the archetypal stories of the Buddha or projecting the duality of Shiva; Black religious thinking matters.

All theological works whether they are Shruti or Smriti are passed from person to person and have a variety of outcomes for those that come into theological and cultural consciousness. The RPS continues to be read, passed on and revered as a religious text and is deserving of recognition.

An Introduction to The Royal Parchment Scroll of Black Supremacy

The Royal Parchment Scroll of Black Supremacy (RPS) is the second of three proto-Rastafari biblical texts that sought to expand the "contours of traditional theology."[1] It is a rendering of a public mythology of Black people in the Americas as well as the private dream of its author, Fitz Balintine Pettersburg. The RPS is a prophetic theological document created out of the misery and suffering of Black people torn from Africa and forced to toil in the New World.

The RPS most prophetic vision is foretelling of the rise of the Ethiopian Kingdom of Haile Selassie I (1930 – 1974) with Diasporic Blacks playing a foundational role in its resurrection: *"So we have the prophetic message more fully*

---

[1]. The two other texts are RA Rogers' *The Holy Piby* (1924) and Leonard Howell's *The Promised Key* (1935).

confirmed. You will do well to be attentive to this as to a lamp shining in a dark place, until the day dawns and the morning star rises in your hearts." (2 Peter 1:19)[2] Foremost, the RPS is a sacred theological text that places Black people at the apex of the development of the body and historical Blackness of Christ. Africa is the mother and creator of humankind and emanating from this creation is the Word, and the Word was with God, and the Word was God. (1 John)[3]

The RPS seeks to address the single most important theological idea of African thought in the Americas: *The Redemption of Africa with Ethiopia at its center.*

Placing Ethiopia at the navel of Black theological consciousness led directly to the placement of the Emperor of Ethiopia Haile Selassie I at the heart of Pettersburg's "poetry of theology." Haile Selassie I ascended to the imperial throne through his paternal grandmother, Woizero Tenagnework Sahle Selassie, who was an aunt of Emperor Menelik II and daughter of Negus Sahle Selassie of Shewa. As such, Haile Selassie I claimed direct descent from Makeda, (Queen of Sheba), and King Solomon of ancient Israel, thus establishing direct descendant to Christ. (2 Samuel 7:14; Ex 4:22 – 23; Hos. 11:1; Ps. 80:15)

Ras Tafari Makonnen Woldemikael was Ethiopia's Regent from 1916 to 1930. Before the publishing of the RPS Ras

---

2. A call to the apostles's to witness to the truth.
3. The prologue of chapter John 1 states the main themes of the Gospel: Life, light, truth, the world, testimony, and the preexistence of Jesus Christ, the incarnate Logos, who reveals God the Father.

An Introduction to The Royal Parchment Scroll of Black Supremacy

Tafari toured Europe and the Middle East visiting Jerusalem, Alexandria, Paris, Brussels, Amsterdam, Stockholm, London, Geneva, and Athens in 1924. This undoubtedly left an indelible impression on the world's African population, including Pettersburg. The sight of a dignified and regal Black African Emperor, motorcading through the streets of Europe gave Black's promise of a new phase of African liberation had begun in Africa. Ras Tafari was and crowned H.I.M. Emperor Haile Selassie I and reigned from 1930 to 1974. H.I.M. Haile Selassie I served as Chairperson of the Organization of African Unity from 1963 to 1964 and 1966 to 1967. Among the Rastafari, H.I.M. Haile Selassie I is revered as the returned messiah of the Bible, a manifestation of God here on earth, an Avatar. The coronation of H.I.M. Haile Selassie I gave Blacks throughout the Diaspora an unambiguous sign of Black royal dignity the world has yet to fully comprehend.

Few documented records survive that can provide an outline of Pettersburg's life. One surviving record indicates that he was born in Kingston, Jamaica in 1897 and died December 11, 1947 in Kingston.[4] Pettersburg wrote The RPS in 1925 or 1926 and that he probably met Marcus Garvey, Leonard Howell and Robert Athlyi Rogers in the United States sometime in 1924. There is no surviving record of the meeting between the men, but undoubtedly there must have been some acknowledgment of the role they would play in shaping an Afrocentric political and religious legacy.

---

4. FHL Film number 001872988.

For nearly 350 years Ethiopianism was *the* guiding ideology for Africans in the Americas seeking to break the bonds of slavery and racial prejudice. Africa's redemption took center stage in the building of life-sustaining African inspired mythologies, a necessity for survival in the Americas. This mythology[5] placed the redemption of Africa at the center of and the primary goal to give Black people so degraded by slavery and colonialism a sense of dignity and purpose. Historically, Ethiopianism was *the* organizing principle preached by Black leaders almost as soon as the first slaves, in defiance of the legal slave system, began to read the Bible. The Bible, replete with images and writings on Ethiopia and coupled with European tales of Prester John,[6] who Europeans believed Ethiopian, made a lasting impression on Black and European collective consciousness. The name Ethiopia was evoked, at various times, and

---

5. The most useful definition of *Public Myth*," "statements about the world and its parts particularly nations and other human in groups that are believed to be true mythology comes from William O'Neill's 1981 Article, "*The Care and Repair of* and acted upon whenever circumstances suggest, or common response required." To provide O'Neill's definition a theological form I have added the following statement: "and brings the individual into accord with the mystic dimension that is the energy consciousness within the Universe."

6. Prester John is a legendary African Christian patriarch and king popular in European chronicles and tradition from the 12th through the 17th century. He was said to rule over a Nestorian (Church of the East) African Christian nation lost amid the Muslims and pagans of the Orient. The accounts are varied collections of medieval popular fantasy, depicting Prester John as a descendant of the Three Magi, ruling a kingdom full of riches, marvels, and strange creatures.

in particular for political purposes to prove that those of African descent were in ancient times a powerful people. Black vindicationists[7] including Robert Athlyi Rogers[8] and Marcus Garvey left a legacy of Ethiopianism that is largely forgotten by a majority of Blacks today. However, to the hundreds of thousands of Rastafari Ethiopianism continues to play a major role symbolically.

The RPS is linked to two religious texts—R.A Rogers' *The Holy Piby* and Leonard Howell's *The Promised Key* because of its their insistence on the central theological role of Ethiopianism and for its poetic and defiant hijacking of the English language (seen as a tool of oppression) to defend Black people from White supremacy. As an example, the RPS runs from seemingly incoherent descriptions:

> *The Book's cover is Limped. The compound impression is the Heart's Block impression. The name of the Book is: Ethiopia's Bible-Text and Rule Book, No. l. (a). Black Supremacy, by His Majesty The King of Kings. (b). Special Notice."*

To an affirmation of a Black liberation theology:

---

7. To Set Free or to Vindicate.
8. Robert Athlyi Rogers (Shepherd Robert Athlyi Rogers), born in Anguilla, was the author of the *Holy Piby*, generally recognized as one of the most important foundational texts in Rastafarian theology. Rogers wrote it for the use of an Afrocentric religion he had founded, known as the *Afro-Athlican Constructive Gaathly*. It was written between 1913 and 1917, and published in 1924. His "Athlican" faith attracted followers, mostly in the West Indies, but never grew to the prominence. Rogers committed suicide on in 1931.

We fully appreciate the Baptism of Black Supremacy, Our Triumph over White supremacy, Our SLAVE MASTER. His and Her Majesty KING ALPHA and QUEEN OMEGA The King of Kings, KNEW The Perfect Value of Holy Baptism UNDER Water, and they taught us how to appreciate The Power of Holy Baptism. It is not surprising that the language of the Royal Parchment has unfolded into what might be called "poetry of theology.

The seemingly intelligible language was used to impart a particular message that challenged Empire. It seems evident that a challenge to White hegemony would in fact necessitate some method of concealment. We have to remember that the 1920's was a particularly repressive period in the United States, Central and South America, Africa and the Caribbean or quite frankly wherever there were Black people. During the early part of the 20th century World War I had been fought over the resources of Africa, the Ku Klux Klan resurfaced to become a major racist's organization in the United States, and European colonial governments were moving to consolidate their hold on their overseas empires. Slavery, racial violence, segregation, apartheid and colonialism forced people of African descent to develop survival skills that necessitated the creative use of language to both confront and disarm the American Oppressor and European Colonial Master. The RPS is an exemplary example of the poetic use of language as a means to assert one's relevance in world affairs and to ward off the forces of religious oppression.

An Introduction to The Royal Parchment Scroll of Black Supremacy

The RPS was a forward thinking text. Along with The Holy Piby and The Promised Key, these three religious texts placed women at the navel of the world (the Axis Mundi) and the epicenter of religious prophesies. Petersburg wrote, "Speaking for the Universe, and the Womanhood of Man, I the Ethiopian woman, is the Crown woman of the world." This is in contrast to Abrahamic religions that often placed women as secondary actors. But let me be clear—the RPS, The Holy Piby and The Promised Key maintain a male centric theological perspective.

The RPS, The Holy Piby, and The Promised Key should be read and understood as a theological trilogy of Black vindication.[9] A few words about The Holy Piby and the Promised Key might be instructive—The Holy Piby written by Robert Athlyi Rogers in 1924 is a remarkable document for its insight and prophecy for the material and intellectual advancement of the Black race and to vindicate the race theologically. Its author Robert Athlyi Rogers was born in Anguilla, British West Indies on May 6, 1891. Athlyi immigrated to the United States in 1913. By 1917 Rogers and his family were residing in Newark, New Jersey.

The theological intent of The Holy Piby is to unite Diasporic Blacks in a holy union of matrimony. Rogers wrote:

---

9. Black Vindication means to set free. It is a field of inquiry in Pan African studies that make an attempt to correct the misleading and false stereotypes of Black people.

And there appeared a light matchless in its beauty. Straightway the whole celestial host shouted and there appeared millions of Angels dancing in the light singing, "Behold! Behold Ethiopia! The bride of the master. Her day has come at last! The Lord had received her hand. Her night has forever passed."

The Lord stretched forth his hands over the earth and there appeared millions of Black men, women and children, who joined with the angles in dancing, singing and rejoicing in the light.

By the time of its publication, the Piby was largely misunderstood as the work of a lunatic. However, over the last few years, there has been renewed interest in *The Blackman's Bible* as The Holy Piby is often referred, particularly among the Rastafari. As Caribbean and Marcus Garvey historian Robert Hill noted the Piby along with the RPS became the interpretive basis of Rastafari ideology.

The Promised Key, written in 1930 by Leonard P. Howell aka G.G. Maragh. Leonard Percival Howell was born in May Crawie, Jamaica on June 16, 1898. Howell's father, Charles Theophilus Howell was both a peasant landowner and tailor and his mother, Clementina Bennett, was an agricultural laborer.[10] In 1918 Howell arrived in Colon, Panama. World War I would have given Howell unprecedented opportunities

---

10. See Robert Hill, *Dread History: Leonard P. Howell and Millenarian Visions on the Early Rastafarian Religion*, (Chicago: Research Associates School Times, 2001), 22 and Helene Lee, *The First Rasta: Leonard Howell and the Rise of Rastafarianism*, (Chicago: Chicago Review Press), 17.

for travel and would have undoubtedly led him to New York. In New York Howell worked at various odd jobs and likely witnessed the social, cultural and political life of the predominately Black section of town Harlem. By 1933 Howell's religious preaching had been in full swing as he worked to speared the word of the divinity of Ras Tafari Makonnen who earlier in 1930 had been crowned Haile Selassie Emperor of Ethiopia in 1930. Howell was one of three men who preached the doctrine that the coronation of Haile Selassie I was the fulfillment of a biblical prophecy of Revelations 5:2-5:[11,12] It is glaringly apparent the text of Howell's Promised Key was largely taken from the RPS.

Between 1900 and 1920 there were a great number of race riots that occurred throughout the U.S. cities including New York City, Atlanta, Georgia; Tulsa, Oklahoma; Springfield, Illinois; and Brownsville, Texas. Whites, in many cases, fought to keep African Americans from competing with them for work or in some cases to simply destroy prosperous Black communities. In 1921 a segregated African American neighborhood in Tulsa, Oklahoma was known as the "Black

---

11. Howell along with Joseph Hibbert, Archibald Dunkley, and Robert Hinds began preaching the idea that Haile Selassie was the Messiah returned to earth. See Robert Hill, *The Marcus Garvey Papers and the Universal Negro Improvement Association Papers, Volume VII*, (Los Angeles: University of California, 1990) 602.

12. "Do not weep. The Lion of the tribe of Judah, the root of David, has triumphed, enabling him to open the scroll with its seven seals." The Lion of the tribe of Judah, the root of David are the messianic titles applied to Christ to symbolize his victory.

Wall Street" for its thriving economic and cultural prosperity, was bombed and burned to the ground by Tulsa's White community in large part because it defied negative stereotypes of Blacks held by Whites. While these acts of racial genocide were meant to destroy Black life whole or in part, these and other bloody race purges of the early 1900s did not kill Black aspirations for justice. In response to White supremacy the National Association for the Advancement of Colored People (NAACP), an African-American civil rights organization, was founded in 1909. Other movements such as the remarkable popularity of Marcus Garvey and his quest for Black Nationalism indicated that the Black masses would not forever contain their frustrated aspirations. As Blacks entered the 1920s the "promised land" prophesied in the old Negro spirituals seemed like far off remnants of an ancient past. Garveyism and other forms of Black Nationalism demonstrated that the long journey to freedom had strengthened, not weakened, their determination to take hold of the promise of the U.S. Constitution or to assert their demands for total liberation and self-rule.

Lastly, I must address the problem of reading and comprehending this and other African Diasporic texts for its spiritual and historical content. Historically, African religions have been devalued by the oppressive society in order to affirm the value of western or Eurocentric religions.[13] So it is necessary that

---

13. See William H. Meyers, "The Hermeneutical Dilemma of the African American Biblical Student," in Cain Hope Felder, (Ed.), *Stony the Road*

we remember that our own sensibilities have been shaped either consciously or unconsciously in ways that condition our own biases. I would not be honest if I did not address the role of European techniques of spiritual interpretation that myself and other Afro western theologians have been trained. These techniques: exegesis, eisegesis, and hermeneutics have shaped the way we theologians have interpreted and continue to interpret all manner of religious texts.

William H. Meyers, Talal Asad, and others have criticized, rather effectively those Eurocentric approaches to the study of Third World and minority cultures as being wholly inadequate. I do not mean to present here new approaches to the study of Afrocentric inspired texts but to remind the reader that they must look to the context of how historical events: slavery, colonialism, segregation, apartheid, and other forms of racial oppression have shaped the religious desires of people of African descent, particularly those in the Afro-Caribbean-American Diaspora.

The reader should be aware that the Christian Bible is the main focus of this and other early 20th-century Black theological discourses. Vincent L. Wimbush wrote, "For the majority of African Americans the Bible has historically functioned not merely to reflect and legitimize piety (narrowly understood), but as a language-world full of stories—of heroes and heroines, of heroic peoples and their pathos and

---

We Trod: African American Biblical Interpretations (Minneapolis: Fortress Press, 1991), 45.

victory, sorrow, and joy, sojourn and fulfillment."[14] Europeans and later Americans shaped the religious, civic and personal identity of African people in the Americas by using the Christian Bible as a means of Christian indoctrination. What Wimbush saw as the "Fourth Reading"[15] (Early Twentieth century to the present) was the development of an esoteric knowledge or principles of interpretation developed to lay claim to an exclusive possession of knowledge of this and other holy books. This application is an outright rejection of western theological norms and practices and the reclaiming of the Bible by carefully reasserting its African origins is the most important of the Fourth Reading's theological acts. Patience, intellectual curiosity, an open mind and heart will serve the reader well in their struggle to comprehend Pettersburg's religious message.

---

14. Ibid, Vincent L. Wimbush, "The Bible and African Americans: An Outline of an Interpretive History," 83.
15. Wimbush describes four major types of "readings" that have been done by African Americans. The four can be found in his essay, ibid.

Guide to the Materials

The RPS is presented in its entirety and also includes an exegesis of the text for study. This work is not intended to be exhaustive but merely to expose those unfamiliar with the RPS to its theology. No grammatical corrections have been made to the original RPS text as it is presented as originally published. Each chapter in the exegesis is laid out in the same format as the RPS for easy reference. The reader should note that at times, Pettersburg spelled his name Petersburg. The variety of spelling has been maintained. Christian, biblical references, when applicable, are taken from the New Revised Standard Version (NRSV) and simply referred to as the Bible. For simplicity the Royal Parchment Scroll of Black Supremacy is simply referred to as RPS and Fitz Ballintine Pettersburg is referred to as Pettersburg.

The Royal Parchment Scroll of Black Supremacy

The Royal Parchment Scroll of Black Supremacy

Our eternal Life Creator The owner of Life, The Eternal Register Office

K.A.Q.O., The Crown

Register General Office Black Supremacy

The Church Triumphant, The Crown Law of Education & Sacred Theocracy

K.A.Q.O.S.W.J.W., The Monarch Documents

(Protect all), Human Descriptions

K.O.K.... The Black man is The Master of this World., Theocracy, The Dictionary,

Law Courts & Money Mints & Governments

K.A.Q.O.... The world's first Triumphant Capital, The isle of Spring, The Triumphant Bible Land, King Alpha and Queen Omega Black Folks ......

His & Her Copyright of Creation,

The Lion & His Lioness & Baby, His & Her Arch Dynasty of Holy Time, His Tri-Divinity & Her Tri-Virginity, His & Her Arch Monarchy, His & Her Majesty Queen

Lula May Fitz Balintine Pettersburg

K.O.K., A.D. 1926, Mt. Africa, The Throne, Ethiopian Bible Owner

A.B.C.

Introduction

My dear inhabitants of this world, we are the foundation stones of the resurrection of the Kingdom of Ethiopia.

Our prayers and labour for your resurrection is past finding out. No Library in this world is able to contain the work of our hands for you.

For we work day and night for your Deliverance.

As for this generation of the 20th Century, you have no knowledge how worlds are built.

And upon what trigger Kingdoms are set.

In my Encyclopedia I will explain to you all, how worlds are being built and what triggers Kingdoms are set on.

I will also explain to you, the Capacities of generations.

Speaking for the Universe, and the Womanhood of Man, I the Ethiopian woman, is the Crown woman of the world.

Without any apology, to any mortal that was ever created by King Alpha and Omega.

I hand you my Rule Book from the poles of Supreme Authority.
I AM THE CANON MISTRESS OF CREATION.
Kingston, Jamaica
B.W.I. Tropic of Cancer
July 15th 1925, A.D.
Rev Fitz Balintine Pettersburg, King of Kings, Creator of Theocracy, and Biblical Sovreign. The Crown Head of Holy Time, A.B.C.—S.J.W.

Ethiopia's Preface

The preface of this Rule Book, is the Finger Post, into the Kingdom of Ethiopia.

Ethiopia is the Succeeding Kingdom of the Angle Saxon kingdom.

Our philosopher is the Angle Saxon Philosopher's (Successor), a wide awake Universal Master Mind.

A man of greater learning is not found on the face of the Globe. A swifter thinker is

God Almighty. A better Christian Soul and King Alpha and Omega. Women must be proud of good men, when they are right on the job.

Men must be proud of us Women when we can deliver able Sons and Daughters to the Four Poles of the Globe.

And make the Nations Hearts rejoice with raging joy. We give God the Glory.

THE CROWN MISTRESS THE THRONE LAW-GIVER. His & Her Majesty King Alpha and Queen Omega, COPYRIGHT.

The Royal Parchment Scroll of Black Supremacy

His & Her Dynasty Queen Lula may Fitz Balintine Pettersburg, S.J.W., A B.C. Ph.D., L.L. ,K.O.K.

Ethiopia's Fly Leaf

ROYAL AIR MOUNT. I am going to teach the Princess to fly around the poles.

PHILOSOPHERS.—Brother Pettersburg and Sister Lula may Butler.

CLERGYMEN.—Bible Owner, Lexium, and Money Mint. My Perfect Air Mount is Black Supremacy, The Church Triumphant. My Dynasty is the Triumphant Dynasty.

We are King Alpha and Queen Omega, THE PAYMASTERS of the World.

Do not forget we are Black Supremacy.

A.B.C. Post Graduates

CHAPTER 1
The Ethiopian Western Philosophy

Now, this is the morning of our resurrection therefore, we the Royal Tree, are very busy, cleaning up our Ancient and Modern Royal right away from Pole to Pole.

And the preparing of Guests for the coronation.

THE CORONATION.—The Coronation of Ethiopia's Postarities are as sure as the purity of pure gold.

THE CROWN MISTRESS.—I Mrs. Indiana Coombs, being the Crown Mrs. of our Ethiopian Repository, for the Tropic of Cancer,

I move the Crownship of the world right at this yard limit of time.

And present this generation of the 20th century my supreme Book of Royal Rules from the Ethiopian Western Repository.

Illustration

Owing to the Universal Rend of our Ancient and Modern Kingdoms, we are at this junction of our history scattered over the Globe into little Sectional groups commonly called Bands.

Ethiopian's Western Repository, is a strictly Christian Museum.

All our local bands throughout the globe, are bent towards this Royal Repository.

THE ROYAL AUTHORITY.—This Official Bill of Royal Authority, is to admit all Bands, Missions, Camps, Denominations, into this Supreme Royal Repository.

THE BALMING MISTRESS.—I being the Balming Mistress of many worlds I charge the Power-House right now.

The Rule Book

The Rule Book leads you into different department of the Kingdom.

The Records of the Kingdom are with us, unto this day.

The regulations, points you to the baseses of the Kingdom.

We move at the Signal of the Trumpet by Degrees call Bands. The Names of the Bands all over the Globe are too numerous to be named.

The Supreme Band, is officially called the Royal Angel Band. The Royal Angel Band is the Crown Band of the world.

THE SEAL OF THE BAND.—The seal of the Royal Angel Band, is the SAMARITAN Woman that needed the pity of Jesus (the well of Samaria) The Order and degree of this Fighting Line is after the Baptism of Jesus, into the Kingdom, by John the Baptist in the Royal River Jordan.

THE SUPREME SIGNAL.—The Supreme Signal is the Official Signal of the (Holy Dove), as she moved from the Mercy Seat and Rested upon King Jesus Head at His Baptism in the Great River Jordan. see Matthew's 3:13.

THE WELL OF SAMARIA.—the Woman at first refused to obey the request of Our Lord because she was spiritually blind.

But when the Great physician opened up her eyes and HEALED her of her infirmities, concerning her many husbands in the City of Samaria, she found out that her five husbands were the five false teachers or denominations throughout the State or Country of Samaria.

Then she cried aloud unto the inhabitants of the city and said "Come see a man that told me all ever I did, and is not a Native of Samaria but an Hebrew, is not this man the very Christ"?

OUR CITIES OF TO-DAY.—Our cities of to-day are inhabited with the self same qualities of people, as it was in the case of Jesus and the woman of Samaria.

CHAPTER 2
The Royal Move

We move at the Signal of the Trumpet by Degrees call Bands. The Names of the Bands all over the Globe are too numerous to be named.

The Supreme Band, is officially called the Royal Angel Band. The Royal Angel Band is the Crown Band of the world.

THE SEAL OF THE BAND.—The seal of the Royal Angel Band, is the SAMARITAN Woman that needed the pity of Jesus (the well of Samaria) The Order and degree of this Fighting Line is after the Baptism of Jesus, into the Kingdom, by John the Baptist in the Royal River Jordan.

THE SUPREME SIGNAL.—The Supreme Signal is the Official Signal of the (Holy Dove), as she moved from the Mercy Seat and Rested upon King Jesus Head at His Baptism in the Great River Jordan. See Matthew's 3:13.

THE WELL OF SAMARIA.—the Woman at first refused to obey the request of Our Lord because she was spiritually blind.

But when the Great physician opened up her eyes and HEALED her of her infirmities, concerning her many husbands in the City of Samaria, she found out that her five husbands were the five false teachers or denominations throughout the State or Country of Samaria.

Then she cried aloud unto the inhabitants of the city and said "Come see a man that told me all ever I did, and is not a Native of Samaria but an Hebrew, is not this man the very Christ"?

OUR CITIES OF TO-DAY.—Our cities of to-day are inhabited with the self same qualities of people, as it was in the case of Jesus and the woman of Samaria.

CHAPTER 3
The Healing Plough Of Creation

The healing plough of the Repository Transplanted and rebuild your very soul and body without fail.

THE MISERY OF THE LAND IS HEALED BY FASTING. We pick you up from out of the midst of the raging misery of the land and HIDE you from the raging Wolves of the land into our Balm Yard.

What is a Balm yard? A balm yard is a Holy place that is wholly consecrated to God Almighty for the cleansing and healing of the Nations. Where the Holy Spirit of God ALONE is ALLOWED to do the Royal Work of Healing.

(Ques.) Who does the Balming work?

(Ans.) Consecrated men and women that the Holy Spirit moves, upon the Blazing Altar of their Souls, and endowed them with power that they command and handle the infirmities of the Nations.

(Ques) Have they any authority from God? (Ans) Yes, we are vessels of the Divine Honour!

(Ques) Have you any authority from the World?

(Ans) ASSUREDLY YES INDEED. The Copyright of Theocracy signs for our destiny and gave us His supreme Affidavit for a Trillion centuries after the end of Eternal Life.

Admission To The Balm Yard

First and last every Soul for admission must believe in the power of the Living God.

Second an admission fee must be paid in advance, from one dollar up. According to the power and DURATION of the MISERABLE infirmities whereof one is afflicted.

SPECIAL NOTICE.

Sometimes I have to perform special medical attention. THE REPOSITORY'S PROPER BODY.

According to the order of Melchisedec the Ethiopian Chief High Priest, we raise the Royal Banner on the top mass of the four poles of Creation, King Alpha and Queen Omega.

CHAPTER 4
Her Royal Banquet

She brought me to her Banqueting House, and her Royal Banner over me, in her Royal Banquet Chamber is love.
THE WORKING OF THE BAND
The Band is a Royal encircling Band.
The Degree of this distinguished Band is a Royal Degree.
The (Encircling) "Staff Officers" are men and women of high spiritual ranks.
A Membership of six (Encircling), "Stax Officials" are sufficient for any one band of one hundred members.
Twenty-five members is one group.
That is one circle.
One circle, only needs one (Encircling) Staff Officer on the parade.
Along with the ORDAINED Circle Mother or Father by law, as many is are in the Banquet O.K.

Royal Notice

Bands are not runned by Ministers. They are runned by the Priesthood, not after the Order of Aaron but strictly after the Royal Order of Melchisedec THE KING OF SALEM.

REVIVALISTS are not common people, if some individuals of the lower order in the dung heap happen to get into the fold by mistake he or she will soon go out and hang him or herself.

The reason why, Revivalists World has not been lightened up with RADIANCE before now, we were waiting for the Delegates of The Resurrection of the Kingdom of Ethiopia.

CHAPTER 5

The Book's Compound Limped Cover

The Book's cover is Limped. The compound impression is the Heart's Block impression. The name of the Book is: and Rule Book, No. 1. (a). Black Supremacy, by His Majesty The King of Kings. (b). Special Notice

I am His and Her Majesty King Alpha and Queen Omega, Our Work is strictly PERFECT.

c. We are not business with Angle-Militant Nakedness.

d. His and Her Triumphant Dynasty, Queen Lula May Fitz Balintine Pettersburg, Owner of Black Supremacy, K.A.Q.O.K.O.K.A.B.C.S.J.W.

CHAPTER 6

Obeah

A Balm yard is not a Hospital

Neither is it an Obeah Shop

Peoples that is guilty of Obeah must not visit a Balm Yard Nor in the Assembly of Black Supremacy.

No admittance for Obeah dogs.

No admittance for FORTUNE-TELLERS and witch and Old Hige.

None whatever, no admittance for GHOST, WITCH, Lizards.

No admittance for Alligators, Snakes, PUSS, Crabs, Flies, Ants, Rats, and Mice, and LODESTONES, and Pins and Needles.

Jan-Crows, The Ravens, and Candles, and Fast Cups, and Rum Bottles, and Grave Yards are not REQUIRED.

People's Clothes, a beast HAIR, and FOWLS and Grave Dirt not wanted.

Eleven, the Woman's Baby will strive in HER BELLY, AND YOUR snake and Lizard will not be able to hurt HER.

For your Ghost will come right back to yourself.

For this is Ethiopia Balm Yard, and we do not have no leprosy.

For Ghost only visit the Lepers Home.

This poison is for ALL Bad Spirits, it is No. 666 it is good for the Pope of Rome and The Monarch of Hell's Bottom.

CHAPTER 7

ETHIOPIA'S BALM YARD POISON NO. 666

You will not plant your Obeah Self, with no Man or Woman, so that they cannot get RID of you until the Obeah ROTTEN.

SCIENCE, MY Dear Obeah King, your Black and White-heart Obeah factory, is upside-down.

Take, this RANKIN Dose of Fatal deadly poison and leave for God Sake; do it quickly. (Supreme Law), K.A.Q.O.K.O.K.

You will not Bline, give big foot or sore, or turn any child ACROSS the Woman's Belly, and Kill her Baby when it is born, or any time after. You will not be there to GRUDGE or OBEAH or rob the people. Nor breed up the Young girls, and treat them like dogs.

Every good looking man's Wife you see, you want to cohabit with her, you rotten GUT SNAKE.

Anywhere a man put a Business, you go there to Kill and Drive Him away, you DEAD COLD HORSE.

This pole is Black Supremacy, King Alpha and Queen Omega.

CHAPTER 8

Perfect Baptism Under Water

Black Supremacy, The Church Triumphant is Perfect Baptism, K.A.Q.O.

We fully appreciate the Baptism of Black Supremacy, Our Triumph over WhiteSupremacy, Our SLAVE MASTER.

His and Her Majesty KING ALPHA and QUEEN OMEGA The King of Kings, KNEW The Perfect Value of Holy Baptism UNDER Water, and they taught us how to appreciate The Power of Holy Baptism.

Now Ethiopia and Africa and Egypt and Vast Creation of Black Supremacy will plant their seeds on the Soil of Black Supremacy. And we have no Pardon to beg Whitesupremacy, no favors to ask her, for she is an ACKNOWLEDGE Deceiver.

From B.C. 4004 to A.D. Second Score, she faked all Christianity.

Black Supremacy The Church Triumphant have Denounced Her openly.

Baptism is a very important Subject to Black Supremacy. Ethiopia is a Baptized Dynasty.

Every Black Man and Woman is Black Supremacy, and must Rush his and her BAPTISM. His and Her Biblical Sovereign Queen Lula May Fitz Balintine Pettersburg, King of Kings.

CHAPTER 9

Perfect Baptism Under Water

Ethiopia is The Dynasty that we have RESURRECTED and baptized INTO Her Own Legal and Divine Body.

According to the Ancient order, His Majesty King Milchispdec and Her Majesty Queen BEULAH—That is to-day, Queen Lula May Fitz Balintine Pettersburg Equinoctial Equinox. The owner of The Land of Corn and Wine. Sacred Songs and Solos, No. 277. The Monarch Songs Book of the World.

Having on the Heart, and my Egyptian Crown and Royal Wrap SAME way A. Al. COPYWRIGHT.

So Ethiopia must find The Virgin Mary and Joseph and Jesus Christ and John The Baptist, my wife and Children, of my own Bodily Loins.

They are all Black Peoples, I, Myself, is His Majesty King Melchisedec, The Said Alpha and Omega, The King of

Kings. To be baptized, in the River NILE, or MY Powerful RIVER JORDAN.

Like as unto Lady Beulah in the Nile, and Lawyer Jesus in the Jordan, is King Alpha and Queen Omega. RIVER BAPTISM, means the Control of The City, as a City, must be Built on a RIVER, Like Egypt The NILE RIVER.

CHAPTER 10
Perfect Baptism Under Water

Palestine My ROYAL JORDON. Notice the Cities and Rivers of the New World.

(To wait at, and on, "POOLS Baptism" in CHURCH BUILDINGS. That is WhitePeople's Leprosy.)

Angle-Militant-Adam-Abraham-Angle-Saxon The Leper. To be Baptized into any of my furious Oceans, ANYWHERE about the Bar of LADY CREATION, is Black Supremacy.

Therefore, all Adamic Abrahamic and Anglo-Saxon "Baptist Churches, "has to WASH Their Hands and Souls, Minds and Hearts from Adam-Abraham-Angle-Saxon, The LEPROUS-PREACHER.

In Countries where it is sometimes COLD, peoples must not be foolish, Jesus Christ WALKED over Sixty Miles to River Jordan to John The Baptist.

When The Ethiopian EUNOCH The BANK MASTER, got to The River, He ASKED "Philip" to Baptize Him. Dump up those Hell-Holes in Churches Called Pools, and Baptize in the River or The Ocean. The Church Triumphant Black Supremacy. WORLD'S CAPITAL.

CHAPTER 11
His And Her Majesty King Alpha And Queen Omega, Marriage Diploma

The Church Triumphant is Black Supremacy. Affidavit, Our Live Eternal Creator, Creator and Almighty God, Crown Arch-Creator of Life.

Terrestrial Affidavit

His and Her Arch-Supremacy of Holy Time, Lover's Firmament and Penetrating, Renovator, Controller, Head and Pillow-Monarch-Groom and Lion-Hearted Virgin Bride.

The Lion and His Lioness, The Greatest Majestic Tri-Virgin Queen Lula May Fitz Balintine Pettersburg Equinoctial-Equinoxes.

Holy Marriage Finger, is Lady Pettersburg's Right Monarch finger.

Head and Pillow Copyright, I can't hurt her, and she cannot hurt me, for we are The Equinoctial-Equinoxes, the Biblical Equator.

Our Professions are, We are The Owner of Communication and Money Mint, Owner of The Human Race, and Operator of Dynasties and Bible House, and Dictionaries.

Mediator, and Crown Head of the Church Triumphant and Black Supremacy.

CHAPTER 12
The Holy Ceremony Of The Mortals

This Triumphant Ceremony, is the Perfect Copy of His and Her Arch Majesty King Alpha and Queen Omega. The Perfect owner of Black Supremacy and Matrimony.

ETHIOPIA'S PERFECT WEDLOCK. His and Her Dynasty, Queen Lula May Fitz Balintine Pettersburg King of Kings, is the Copyright and FOUNDER of the Ethiopian Virgin Dynasty, YOUR WEDLOCK.

She cannot hurt him, and He cannot hurt her. She can have him, and He can have her on the Train of Time, for they are HEAD and Pillow, heart and SOUL Companion for life.

The Church Triumphant, and Black Supremacy, has nothing at all to do with Whitesupremacy, and the church militant, MARRIED IS EASED talk.

Adam, The Leper, and Abraham the Lunatic, are the Directors of the Marriage Proclamation of the Church Militant and WhiteSupremacy. RICHER for POORER,

BETTER FOR WORST, UNTIL DEATH. That is White-supremacy is marriage Solemnization. Adam The Leper, and Abraham The Indomitable.

CHAPTER 13

Ceremony Of The Mortals

MORTALS, you follow me, I will show you where the Marriage Office is Perfect Ceremony, is Black Supremacy.

"The Monarch Finger" on your (Right Limb is, Holy Union's finger).

Both (male and Female), will stand facing Each other at the Matrimonial Tribunal, and The Marriage officer will (Read) to them My (Perfect Crown Document).

And say to my Guest, According to The Perfect Copy, of His and Her Arch Majesty King Alpha.

You are now equal, HEAD and Pillow-Heart and SOUL Life-HOLD COMPANION.

She cannot hurt you, and you cannot hurt her, she cannot leave you on Earth, and you cannot get to Heaven without her.

Your ring is an emblem of Loyalty, To The Perfect Tree of Life. Thus saith Our Creator The Living God.

By Perfect Ceremony, The Church Triumphant and Black Supremacy.

The Royal Parchment Scroll of Black Supremacy

A Royal Child Christmas Gift. (9.O.C.NIGHT) FROM THE CIRCLE THRONE THE KING OF KINGS.

CHAPTER 14

Fasting—How To Fast

I am His Majesty King Alpha, The King of Kings, The Copyright of Creation, The First and The Last.

Blessed are they that SEARCHETH the DEEP THINGS ON THE TREE OF LIFE for my Wisdom is DEEP and is past finding Out.

Thus Saith the Living God, Owner of Life.

To Over Come WhiteBondage and filth and Black Hypocrisy, amongst your Own Black Skin, you HAVE TO FAST HARD.

For the Whiteman is very filthy, and The Black man is an Hypocrite.

An Hypocrite means a crook, a filthy man is that class of WhiteFolks that cuts with the Crook.

They are called Black White.

Ye are the light and Salt of this and Other Worlds. Always have a BASIN of FINE OR COARSE SALT on your Fast TABLE as long as God is your RULER.

When you break your fast do not THROW the WATER over your heads, the trouble will fall on you. When you are all ready, with your Cup in your hand, the ELDER WILL ASK "IS IT ALL WELL"!

Every body shall say together, "all is well with me". Then the Elder shall ask again, "who will bear a true witness for the: Tree of Life"?

All shall say "by the Living God I will, God Helping Me, for Life". And The Leader, Shall say follow me with your Cup of Troubles, to the BURRYING PLACE of sin and shame.

Then Every Body walk quietly and RESPECTFULLY throw away the Water.

Then come in and wash your hands and face in a Basin of SALT AND WATER.

Then brake your real fast and be happy, feeling SATISFIED and REVIVED and Lovely.

House to House Fasting is very Powerful, it lifts the Work and REMOVES Devils from the Homes of those in DISTRESS.

Once Per week for the General Assembly is alright. A LOVE Feast (Fast) every 3 or 6 months is NEEDED.

CHAPTER 15

The Egyptian Copyright Department

His and Her Dynasty Queen Lula May Fitz Balintine Pettersburg, K. A. Q. O., are Egyptians, The Ethiopian Kingdom Master. And the Shepherd and Mrs. Habakkuk and. Lady Indiana his Mother, are Ethiopians, the former Owner of the State of Indiana, United STATES OF AMERICA.

And His-Majesty King Noah The Owner of Mt. Newark, New Jersey. And Ellen Park Johnson,, the Mrs. of New Orleans. And Mt. Africa, The World's Capital, the New Bible land, The Triumphant Lot is my own lot until This Day.

Slave Traders, CALLED the WORLD'S CAPITAL, Jamaica, British West Indies.

His Majesty King Joseph is Owner of the Great Sea, and Lady Pettersburg, The Atlantic Ocean until This Day. Canada and the furious Mississippi I have no intention to give away. Neither my

PEACEFUL Pacific OCEAN PLAINS as long as God Almighty Lives. Great ARTIC and Atlantic swellings belongs to LAWYER JESUS.

KING ALPHA AND QUEEN OMEGA Copyright of Holy Time, January 8th 1926.

BLACK SUPREMACY KING OF KINGS

CHAPTER 16
SPEAKING IN DIVERS TONGUE

Before the Adamic DEADLY DISEASES poisoned The Human family with FALLEN ANGLES Blue MURDER.

There has been only one PERFECT language on the FACE of the Globe.

Therefore, the Angle-Militant fallen Angles' tongues, are not appreciated by His Majesty the Monarch of Life.

Thus saith the Living God to Creation VAST. For they have deceived the Race man.

And have killed the Mortal SUPREME Monarch. Heaven is no GUESSOR, long before this World was, Heaven has BEEN running co-trillions of CENTURIES ago.

Ethiopia's Repository will Change and qualify the fallen Angels Deadly POISONOUS INDOMITABLE Lying tongues.

STUPIDITY is the most they get out of the Various tongues spoken by the Majority.

The Royal Parchment Scroll of Black Supremacy

Ninety five out of every HUNDRED do not know what they do or say. And Ghost can fool them at any corner. (Ruth and Lillian) said they knew what they are talking about.

CHAPTER 17
SPEAKING IN TONGUES

Professor Rogers The House of Athlyi.

One fallen Angel, told Professor Rogers, that his name is (Douglas). And Poor Rogers did not know, he was "The Principal of Hell". Judge Lucifer The Devil is no Common Theologian.

He has got PASTOR RUSSEL and Judge Rutherford Dead.

FOOLED with His Doctrine. Called Millions Living Now, under Adam-Abraham-Angle-Saxon The Leper, SHALL NEVER DIE. Note: (Millions Living now shall Never Die).

In Nineteen Twenty-two I told Judge Rutherford he must stop preaching Lies.

The Apostle PAUL CALLED them Principality.

The Pilot Marcus Garvey. The fallen Angel, whose name is Lady Astonishment.

The Royal Parchment Scroll of Black Supremacy

She told Pilot Garvey, That her Big Universal Name is The Universal Negro Improvement Association and African Communities League.

The Pilot Believed the Angle-Militant Upside Down Queen. Special Notice.

I am ready to tell you, That Lady Creation Vast is BLACK SUPREMACY. His and Her Majesty King Alpha and Queen Omega, are Black Dignitary. By Lady Pettersburg Equinoctial-Equinox Founder of Mortal Speech.

Speak with MORTALS, not Angels, King Alpha and Queen Omega K.O.K.

CHAPTER 18

My Rain Bow Circle Throne

His and Her Arch Sovereign of Holy Time Queen Lula May Fitz Balintine Pettersburg. Equinoctial-Equinox, Owner of the Rain-bow. Our UNIVERSAL THRONE must be DECKED right to the Canopy, from my Equator, to the CIRCLE BRIDGE.

Heaven is not guessing The Eternal Government Business. I am Philosopher, Copyright, Lawgiver and Clergyman.

Bible owner, Lexicographer, Surveyor General of Creation and Owner of Money Mint.

The Rain-Bow will not speak in this Port, She has Her CHAMBERLOIN. His Tri-Divinity and Her Tri-Virginity, K.A.Q.O.

The Laws Of Perfect Resurrection

The Ethiopian Crown Mrs. at Canon Port, is a Noble Philosophist. A Virgin must always be look for at every Resurrection.

Wherever a King is, there must be a VIRGIN QUEEN. Kings are not allowed to MARRY any one but a VIRGIN QUEEN in Order of Perfect Dynasty, a PERFECT STANDARD.

CHAPTER 19
Ethiopia's Triumphant Proclamation

The Bible Owner, of Holy Time, DENOUNCED The Bible Militant.

Also The Militant Dictionary.

And take off the Black Man and his Posterities from off The Angle-Militant SLAVE-TRAIN at Nationality.

And Planted the Church Triumphant, The Black Supremacy on The Triumphant Soil of the World's Capital, The New Bible Land, The Isles of Spring.

The same Country, That The Anarchy called, Jamaica, British West Indies.

Black Supremacy's Greatest Men and Women are Sub-Ways and AIR-MASTERS of every SHADE.

They Sleep in BED and Eat WITH you, and you do not KNOW what TRIGGER your LIFE and destiny is ON.

The Gods of Laws are my Students.

The Air you are breathing This Minute is Mine.
The BABWIRE Eternity is Mine.
The Brim-stone and Fire, Vulcannon is Mine.
Every Thunder and Lightening is Mine.

I want you to know that the (indomitable firmament is Mine.)

When I speak to her she OBEY MY ROYAL VOICE.

His and Her Majesty King Alpha and Queen Omega and Lady Pettersburg, King of Kings.

CHAPTER 20
The Royal Swaddling Of Jesus And John The Baptist

John The Baptist wears The Monarch's GIRDLE about his loins.

And Jesus Christ wore the Supreme Swaddling, Both loins and head.

And we, Black Supremacy, wears them The Three ways.

First on Our heads The Royal Wrap, (12 yards) King of Kings. The MONARCH'S GIRDLE, the first to the Skin, Through the Rectum on both legs, closely fitted and all around the waist. Both MALE and FEMALE for life, DAY AND NIGHT.

Ethiopia must do the Same for life, and Safe-Guard your Dynasty, and Black Supremacy, The Church Triumphant, K.A.Q.O.K.O.K.

I AND MY CREATOR ARE ONE in PURPOSE, as MY Boy Jesus said he and I are one, the True Vine, and I the

Husband-MAN His Tri-Divinity and Queen Lula Pettersburg, Her Tri-Virginity My Head and Pillow companion, K.A.Q.O.K.O.K.

This is Officially called the MONARCH CROWN WRAP. Place of Writing, from the THRONE World's Capital The Bible House in The Furnace ROOM.

January 10, 1926 A.D. 2000. (4 O.C.P.M.)

CHAPTER 21

The Load-Stone Lepor

The Load-Stone Lepor from Nationality, is running towards my dynasty.

Just give him Ethiopia's Balm Yard No. 666 instantly, K.A.Q.O. Give his business to the Monarch of Disgrace.

A Load-Stone God, left me standing, outside the boor, just after he draw out the last 10 in my pocket with his Load-Stone.

No Pardon for you Rev. Load Stone Jesus at the Cross. Get off this Train and Wash your SOUL is the Vengeance of God's Eternal Wrath.

They uses Load-Stone into The Militant Bible House, for that is a House of Science, The Chief Obeah Shop on Militant Precipice.

They Called themselves Scientist to Obeah Pinnacle. Rev. Bishop Load-Stone Honourable and Medical Robber, dogs can be your WIFE and Puss can be your Self.

The Royal Parchment Scroll of Black Supremacy

You said you deal with puss, for puss has nine lives, but I am the Keeper of The Tree of Life.

And all puss gutts, belongs to me.

Lepors do not dictate to me.

His and Her Monarch King Alpha and Queen Omega. King of Kings.

CHAPTER 22

The Law Of Resurrection

According to the RULE of Resurrections (one Race) of people must go down to dishonour, and The Other to Honour.

Caution

Make your INDIVIDUAL way Straight, when you are at THE head of AFFAIRS with GOD for HEAVEN DO NOT PAY, every WEEK.

But your Due-bill is SURE for every minute of your life. I am His and Her Majesty King Alpha and Queen Omega The Pay Master for the Terrestrial Bar.

Black Supremacy is the Queen of Ethiopia's Triumphant Resurrection.

Africa's DESIRE is to Rebuild Solomon's Temple, but Solomon, is not BIG ENOUGH, nor his FATHER DAVID to dictate to the Monarch of Dread Creation.

I am Building a World's Super Capital for The Church Triumphant, The Black Supremacy at the World's Dam-Head.

I am the Master Builder of Continents, and Countries, DYNASTIES and Kingdoms on this Earth PLAIN. I am The Perfect Royal Head of This World, The Root of Creation King Alpha and Queen Omega, The First and The Last.

CHAPTER 23
Ethiopia's Banqueting Chamber

Lady Black Supremacy, The Church Triumphant INVITED me into her Royal Banqueting Universe.

May Be, you might find a Royal Lover for your Own Heart in This Banquet, at this LOVE SEARCHING Battle GROUND.

If you do, let us know, when it ripe.

At the Banquet in Egypt, King Solomon, The Black Man, made love, with King Pharaoh The Black man's virgin princess.

A BANQUETING CHAMBER, HAS MANY ROYAL SECTIONS.

You may have a Thanks-Giving Banquet for Marriage Life.

A Memorial Banquet for a Member gone to REST.

You will also have a Banquet of Black Supremacy.

Banquet for CHILD'S BIRTH. New Home or Business, or for Sick Recovery.

The Royal Parchment Scroll of Black Supremacy

For a Friend, or, An Assembly.
For Souls Having Peace with GOD.
For New Year, Xmas and HOLIDAYS.
For Business Properties.
For Advertising your Business.
For King Alpha and Queen Omega.
A Love Banquet to The Glory of God.

CHAPTER 24

Government

Black Supremacy has taken Charge of Whitesupremacy, K.A.Q.O.

Instead of Our Saying, Civilization, hereafter we (all) shall say Black Supremacy.

Just take this Drench of INDOMITABLE Fury and Move for the Church Triumphant right from the Bridge.

Black Supremacy is the Church Triumphant.

Black Supremacy will promote the Mortals of every SHADE according to YOUR power to go.

The Black MUSEUM will open Day and Night for Life.

Education will be free, and Compulsory, to all Mortals Being.

You may go to SCHOOL UNTIL YOU DIE, if you are not an enemy to Black Supremacy and The Church Triumphant. Men and Women can Marry Right in School if you are of a RESPECTABLE proportion of Dignity, BLACK

MUST NOT MARRY WHITENOR WHITEBLACK, "RACE ENMITY."

Always be a RESPECTFUL DIPLOMAT.

Always give an intelligent reply to every person that Approach, or write you on any subject.

Always ask for the full value, INSIDE NATURE, of any Written Subject.

Do not put your quick judgment on any person.

Confidence is not quick to move.

Just what a people are, that is just the State of your Government.

Do not follow Court House and Doctors, they will fake you to Death.

Do not marry any Divorce person, it is a curse to you. Stick to your own Wife or Husband.

Do not WATCH and PEEP your WIFE or HUSBAND, you are only digging a grave for your self. Do not try to let your Wife, or Husband, or Family feel small, because you got more College filth in your HEAD.

Hold Them up, they are the cause of you being what you are.

I KNOW thousands of College hogs and dogs and PROFESSIONAL Swines!

Also some very FINE peoples.

WHO ARE THOU? STEP ON YOUR SIDE.

His Majesty King Alpha and, Queen Omega and Lady Pettersburg. THE GOVERNMENT.

CHAPTER 25
The Owner Of Most Holy Theocracy, K.A.Q.O.

His and Her Arch-Sovereign of Perfect Time, King Alpha and Queen Omega.

The Perfect Husband and Wife Theocracy, His and Her Biblical Equinox. Her Monarch, Queen Lula May Fitz Balintine Pettersburg, The Crown Head of Holy Time and Pay Master of Holy Theocracy, The Owner of Money Mint, and Keeper of The perfect Tree of Life.

The Right Master of Terrestrial Bequest, King Alpha and Queen Omega.

The Royal Copy Queen Lula May Fitz Balintine Pettersburg, K.A.Q.O.K.O.K.C.L.C. Surveyor, and Patten Master of BEQUEST, Ph.D.L.L.D.A.B.C.S.J.W. Post Graduate, "The Will" MASTER of CREATION.

AND OWNER of COMMUNICATION, AND ROYAL FOUNDER.

World's Capital, new Bible land, The Triumphant Lot
The Isles of Spring, January 11. 7.15.A.M. 1926. A.D. 2000
IN THE FURNACE ROOM.

CHAPTER 26
World's Building

The Root and Foundation of World's Buildings is by Communication.

Heaven is Runned by Communication. The Wisdom of GOD DEPENDS on Communication.

January 10, 1926, A.D. 2000, His Monarch, Victor, Communication is Lady Pettersburg's First born.

And Lady Triumph the Second.

Must not be seen before, The 12. Tri-Virgin Equinoctial Equinox. CELESTIAL LAW A.B.C.S.J.W.K.O.K.K.A.Q.O. January 12 (9.O.C.A.M.). WORLD'S CAPITAL COPYRIGHT OF HOLY TIME.

TO HIS MONARCH, VICTOR, COMMUNICATION AND HIS SISTER LADY TRIUMPH.

I am The Monarch of Creation, Your Perfect Father, I am writing to you today before you are being CONCEIVED in The WORLD in your Mother's Belly.

Lady Pettersburg the Perfect Mrs. of BLACK SUPREMACY is my Wife, Your Mother, is a perfect lady.

I married Her, through Communication in the copyright Department at The World's Capital, and could not TELL what part of the Globe, she was at the time.

And Seal Her Married Diploma behind her Back, because she is Queen Omega and I am His Majesty King Alpha the King of Kings.

CHAPTER 27
World's Building

And up to the Hour, January 12, your Birth Day, I have not had a line from her, for the Anarchy, The Angle-Militant Supremacy, at Nationality will not allow her to Communicate with me.

For they was ruling the Port of Communication, and they will not allow her to CROSS The Angle-Militant Gulf.

Plant that as you go, from Generation to Generation, as Long as God Lives.

And She and I, are The Keepers of The Tree of Life and Creation's Wisdom and Power House, and Money Mint is ours, for life.

And children must INHERIT their PARENTS WEALTH.

That is why they tries to Kill you in your Mother's Belly. Have nothing to do with the Anarchy: Do not allow Black Supremacy to Marry any one from Whitesupremacy. for there is a Rock BOTTOM OFFENCE, CALLED SLAVERY in the Heart of WhiteFolks that will come up in one NIGHT.

He will put you and his own WIFE to sleep in his bed, and let you cohabit with her all you want just to get you in.

He will worship you, just to get on top of your Belly.

Emily MCGHIE (said), WhitePeoples Mind is the Snake's Mind. Before I trust a WhitePerson, I trust a Snake.

They take your LIFE with their PRIVATE INTO YOUR PRIVATE. (Last Warning)

CHAPTER 28
General Marcus Garvey and Bishop Rogers

Pilot Marcus Garvey, warrants the Black Slaves at Nationality to leave for the Ethiopian's Yard Limit. Through the instrument of (Lady Astonishment). PHILOSOPHICAL COMMON SWITCH.

The EUROPEAN LONG-DISTANCE ITALIAN-JEWISH-ANGLO-TORPEDO. Called the Universal Negro Improvement Association and African League.

His Holiness Pope Rodgers, The House of Athlyi, The Athlican's Piby, a good little MESSENGER. Lady G.J. Garrison and Professor W.D. Davis, Met me at The World's Capital With the "Little Piby". Rev. and Mrs. Charles Goodridge is gone with the Message. Rev. W.R. Carter and His Sister ADDE is also on the ROUTE. Professor John Wilson Bell. Doctor of Angle-Militant-Theology, was Master of Ceremony at No. 7 Bond Street, Kingston

Jamaica, A.D. (1924). I was Ordained by Him for MILITANT BATTLE-FIELD.

But I leaped The Militant Biblical Gulf, K.A.Q.O.K.O.K. I poled Whitesupremacy, That said Year.

I promoted Doctor Bell to the Rank of Kings for the Mistake he made.

CHAPTER 29
The Eternal Law Office

HIS AND HER MAJESTY KING ALPHA AND QUEEN OMEGA'S WEDDING, K.A.Q.O.K.O.K.

St. Matthews 25 (ten) 10th Verse, left words, for Me to Lock Out Adam-Abraham-Angle-Saxon the Lepor from my wedding's Banquet. I do not Call Ministers for they are not working for me, they are following Adam-Abraham-Angle-Saxon the Lepor.

Legislators said one Man CANNOT serve two Masters. Adam-Abraham The lepor are Ministers and Lawyers Boss.

For all they teach and Preach about is Adam and Eve and Abraham The Lepor.

For they do not see not (even) one Book in The Bible, written by Adam and Eve, or the Book of Abraham, or Book of Isaac According to the (CLEARNESS) of This case, there is nobody name Adam and Eve, and Abraham The Lepor, if you want to get away with RED HOT MURDER.

The Royal Parchment Scroll of Black Supremacy

If you ever touch the Slave papers they catch you as sure as God Lives. S.J.W.K.A.Q.O.K.O.K.

CHAPTER 30

The Soldiers At Camp and Police Dept.

The Officers and Soldiers at Camp that has power and influence are WELL POSTED.

Their names you will not know.

Every Police Department is out there. K.A.Q.O.K.O.K. LEGISLATORS SAID, ONE MAN CANNOT SERVE TWO MASTERS.

Ministers says they can't work with Adam and Eve, and work for His and Her Majesty King Alpha and Queen Omega the same time. Abraham the Historian SAID DISPISE the both of them and follow him.

Lawyers said, you have got to find a fault with them.

The Judge said, LEAVE The Alpha and Omega out because they are Black and, SKIN FOR SKIN.

CHAPTER 31
Black Supremacy's Infant's Diploma

Lady Pettersburg's infant's Triumphant Diploma. By His and Her Majesty King Alpha and Queen Omega, for Black Supremacy.

Name.
Date. Month Year
Address.
Mothers.
Age.
Father.
Age.
Profession.
Race.
Continent.
Clergyman.
Name of Monarch.
Name of the Chief Lady.

Name of Chief Physician.
Name of The Arch Bishop of Creation (Not Nation.)
Name of the Chief of Education.
Name of the owner of Communication.
Name of the Owner of Bible – House and Money Mint.
HEAVEN'S LAW BOOK

CHAPTER 32

His And Her Monarch the African Potentate

The Lesson learnt by Slave Traders through Black Histories is well PRESERVED.

We have given Our Blood, Souls, Bodies, and Spirits to REDEEM Adam-Abraham-Angle-Saxon the Whiteman from his DREADFUL downfall and Leprosy, but from 4004 B.C. to A.D. SECOND SCORE at his astonishing stop.

He is STILL INFESTED with the indomitable INCURABLE accursed Deadly Diseases.

We have given him access to the Tree of Life, we gave him the Garden of Eden, we gave him Egypt, Palestine, Africa.

We gave him The Life, Soul, and Body of Jesus Christ, at the Request of the Lepor, Ciaphas, their Chief Priest. We gave them Daniel and The Body of the Black Virgin, The Mother of Jesus, and they took Joseph also.

We gave ourselves to be Slaves for Hundreds of Years.

WE GAVE UP KING ALPHA AND QUEEN OMEGA, THE FIRST AND THE LAST.
Now we are Perfectly DISGUSTED OF THEM.
We wash our hands of THEM, for life.

CHAPTER 33

Ethiopia's School, College & University

Crown Law for Schools, Colleges, and Universities on earth. His and Her Creative and Majestic Arch-Sovereigns King Alpha and Queen Omega, Pay Master of Creation. Revelation 22.

Chap 12-13 Verses. This Lesson, and these Lessons, are written by my own hand from my Circle Throne, at the Judgment Pole, December 12th 1925 A.D. 2000.

Special Explanation. His Majesty King Alpha and Queen Omega are not Our Creator HIMSELF.

They are Our Creator's PAY MASTER and BOOK-KEEPER on the Train of Holy Time, and Keeper of the Most Holy Tree of Life.

Our Live Creator is, the Creator of Life, and Master of all. S.S.S.S.S.

Our Eternal Creator, is Creator and Owner of The Perfect Tree of Life.

The Tri-Divinity, and Her Tri-Virginity King Alpha and Queen Omega, are Man and Wife, (commonly) called "Alpha and Omega" we are Black Peoples.

God called the First Man Alpha, and the Second Alphabet, And told us that we are (Omega). So The Trinity was IMMEDIATELY Created.

So WE USED, The Holy ALPHABET as Our Medium of Communication, that is why we are the Owner of Education, and First and Last, Communicator.. S.S.S.S. A.B.C.—X.Y.Z

Now Our First Names Alpha, and Her Alphabet, or Alpha and Omega is (Victory).

"Our Last Names, are on Our pay-roll." Revelation 22.C. 12-13 Verses.

His and Her Triumphant Virgin Dynasty.

Queen Lula May Fitz Balintine Pettersburg, Owner of Money Mint and Bible House and The Human Family.

Supreme Judge of Creation, and Arch Bishop of Holy Time.

Copyright Philosopher, Clergyman, Law-Giver. S.S.S.S Form of Christian Worship.

The Black Peoples Triumphant Baptist Assembly. No. 1. S.S.S.S. (Certified Married Officers).

The WhitePeoples Baptist Brotherhood. No. 2. S.S.S.S.

CHAPTER 34
Black Supremacy's Patten Officer

His and Her Arch Monarch Sovereign of Holy Time, King Alpha and Queen Omega.

His and Her Black Supremacy, Queen Lula May Fitz Balintine Pettersburg, Arch Bishop and Supreme Judge (Virginity and Divinity of Holy Time".

Owner of COMMUNICATIONS and all Creations OLD AND NEW.

CREATOR of HOLY GENEALOGY, Owner of THEOCRACY LEXICOGRAPHY AND MONEY MINT.

Creator of Furious Dynasties and Kingdoms, OPPERATORS and RUNNER.

The Crown Head of Most Holy Time and Keeper of the Tree of Life and Perfect Majestic Matrimonial Sovereignty.

Mediator of Celestial and Terrestrial PERFECT CORDIAL.

REGISTRATION LAW BLACK SUPREMACY, KING ALPHA & QUEEN OMEGA.

All Governments and "PROFESSIONS" must be REGISTERED in The Royal OFFICE of Black Supremacy. Starting from the World's Capital throughout, Lady Creation. All Professionals Pattern of Pure Nature, can be moved for 21 years before a New Registration is REQUIRED. HIS AND HER MONARCH BLACK SUPREMACY, Lady Pettersburg, K.A.Q.O., KING OF KINGS.

CHAPTER 35

Eve, The Mother Of Evil

The Adamic Tree of Knowledge and Eve the Mother of Evil. Genesis 2nd Chapter.

The Adamic Apple Tree. My dear Lepor, your name is Adam-Abraham-Anglo-Saxon, Apple Tree.

That looks pretty and respectable to your eyes. Don't it? Why: Yes indeed—GROSS Beauty is The QUEEN IN HELL; and the Royal Lepor.

Adam and Eve, and Abraham, Anglo-Saxon peoples-are all White. s.s.s.s. I am his and her Arch sovereign of Most Holy Time, His and Her Perfect Virginity, King Alpha and Queen Omega, His and Her Dynasty Queen Lula May Fitz Balintine Pettersburg, Owner of Creation.

We are Black Supreme Crown Head of Most Holy Time, The Pay Master and Keeper of The Perfect Tree of Life.

We are Creators of Creation. Dynasties and Kingdoms, Holy Genealogy and Holy Theocracy, and Celestial and Terrestrial Mediator if you wish to know Our Professions.

CHAPTER 36

The Eternal Come Back

King Alpha and Queen Omega's Eternal Come Back.

His Majesty and His Wife, Queen "Bulah" May Fitz Balintine Pettersburg. King of Kings. "Egyptian Chestnut" Winner. My Dear Creation, I am His Monarch Sovereign, Pay Master and Owner of this World.

Just make one Eternal come Back at my Pay Office. Mrs. Lula May Fitz Balintine (Bulah Pettersburg, K.A.Q.O.)

Please "Madam", your Vehement Venerable Pay Mrs., "My friend Omega," of Old Alpha the Lion of Creation.

Please hand me, the "Pay Roll" and The Militant Balance Sheet.

And your "Majesty" will mount my Exceeding Great Circle Throne, and throw Old Theocracy above the wheel of Holy Time, right into Holy Eternity, to the Lion of Alpha and Omega. King Affidavit "O.F." "O.F." of Forevermore."

The Militant Pay Cheque is, King Alpha and His Wife's Eternal come Back.

The Militant Abraham is guilty of Eternal-Leze-majesty, S.S.S.S., A.D. 1925.

CHAPTER 37

None Matrimonial Prosecution

CRIME OF NONE, MATRIMONIAL LEZE MAJESTY (MATRIMONIAL PROSECUTION.) (Act.) 7377. SPANISH TOWN, English Jamaica (Record office)

Adam-Abraham-Angle-Saxon, the Indomitable Lepor and his Harlot, Eve and Sarai, and Keturah was driven out of my (Virtuous) Dynasty by myself, since B.C. 4004, for fornication and THEFT.

My SACRED Chronicle, dated B.C. 4004 and my Great Chronological Fifty Horse Power-Printing Press. I am that said Man that Adam-Abraham and his boy CAIN & ABLE CUT to pieces and took My Royal Printing Fifty Horse Rower Press, and pattern it and call it The Chronicle Printing Press. His "Whoredom" is Recorded in First Chronicle, 1st Chap 32, etc.

And more than that, Adam-Abraham-Angle-Saxon, was never MARRIED, nor any That followed that Lepor.

For up to October 17, 1925, I requested the General Register Office in Spanish Town, Kingston, Jamaica, for Adam-Abraham-Angle-Saxon "Certified Marriage Officer's Diploma" (This World's Strongest Document).

Reply, October 21st, 1925 (Letter Number 7477). Sir you requested me to send you (Certified Marriage Officer's Diploma.) In reply to say, Adam-Abraham-Angle-Saxon-Office does not supply such documents.

To The Rev. Fitz Balintine Pettersburg, Ph.D,.L.L.D., October 21, 1925. A.D., Post Script.

The Slave Owners Children, they has a little SLIP OF PAPER into the Office of Slave City Official TROUSERS Pockets in the FARMS.

That is all we think of their Official Names and Denominations, O.K. Notice.

That is called Non-Matrimonial Leze Majesty.

Supreme Action. His and Her Triumphant Dynasty, His and Her Monarch Black Supremacy, Crown Marriage Dynasty, of Lady Creation, King Alpha and Queen Omega.

CHAPTER 38

His And Her Majesty King Melchiszedek's Affidavit

The Egyptian Supreme Lady, Lady Bulah, The Royal Chestnut Winner, Creation's Greatest Songsters, The Lioness of Alpha and Queen Omega, is my Head and Pillow, Heart and Soul, Wife, if you please.

We are Black Peoples, if you please; we are only called the Exodus, if you please; (The Book of Exodus) is mine, if you PLEASE.

Notice if you see Moses and Aaron and Abraham, gave any (Strong) report of me in their fake Bible, if you please.

I, Personally, am His Majesty King Alpha, the King of Kings, if you please; the World's PAY MASTER, if you please.

I am only an Eternal Government Employee, I got REWARD for Her Majesty Queen Omega, Wife of His Majesty King Alpha, the King of Kings, for Her Tri-Virginity, Creation's Womb-Carrier.

January 3rd (5.O.C.P.M.) His work of Six thousand years, from B.C. 4004 to 5.O.C.P.M. January 3rd 1926.

The Old Testament has no Book in Abraham's name, not even one like (Obadiah).

The Man with the one (tallent). Obadiah was a SLAVE in King Ahab's House, yet he could make the efforts to write one called the Book of Obadiah.

Special Notice

So therefore, as far as Old Testament Books are concerned from Genesis to Malachi, are (39) Work-Men and Women.

(Ruth and Queen Estha) among the men on gospel journey. Well SINCE a man has right to pay without Work, this world can also work with pay.

CHAPTER 39
New Testament Port

There is no Book of Isaac, nor his Father Abraham in the New Testament. Father, most sacred and Ever Living God, Heaven and Earth's Creator.

And there's is no "Book" in the Bible for the Anglo-Saxon Creation, Most Living and Eternal and Ever Living Sovereign, Owner of Life.

Adam-Abraham-Angle-Saxon, is not entitled to any ETERNAL. Revelation 22, 12-13.

I am your Eternal Pay Master on the Train of Holy Time YOUR JOINT AIR and Keeper of The Tree of Life, Your FRIEND.

His Majesty King Alpha and Queen Omega, His and Her Dynasty of Melchiszedek, of Her Monarch Queen Lula May Fitz Balintine Pettersburg, King of Kings.

The Book of His and Her Biblical Sovereign Queen Lula May Fitz Pettersburg Pay Master pf Holy Time.

His Majesty King MELCHISEDEC'S AFFIDAVIT.

CHAPTER 40

The Ethiopian People's Ordination

My dear Ethiopia, Creation Vast, is now Ethiopian Triumphant Dynasty.

The Ethiopian is the CROWN HEAD of this Earth Field since Heaven and Earth has been BUILT by the Living God.

Thank and Praise the Ever Living God, as long as Eternal Ages Roll.

We are your Parents, His and Her Triumphant Dynasty, King Alpha and Queen Omega, the Keepers of The TREE OF LIFE. We are not any family at all to Adam and Eve and Abraham and Isaac, and the Anglo-Saxon Slave-Owners.

For that is exactly how His Majesty King Noah the Black Monarch was DROWN at Antediluvia by Adam-Abraham, THE ANARCHY.

Judge Samson lost his TRIBUNAL and his life by marrying the Philistine Whitewoman. See Judges 14, 15 & 16 Chapters.

See the Philistines Judges plotting out RIDDLES with the woman how to get him.

CHAPTER 41
No. 1. The Bible Editor

HIS & HER BLESSED PSALMS OF KING ALPHA AND QUEEN OMEGA.

His & Her Holy Theocracy, His & Her Psalmist, The Head of the World.

His Tri-Divinity & Her Tri-Virginity Queen Lula May Fitz Balintine Pettersburg of Holy Theocracy.

MY DEAR TREE OF LIFE, DEAR HEART, My True-Hearted Wife, I am just ready to put Out David the Chaff, Psalm 1st Ver. 4. The Owner of the Psalms, is The Blessed Virgin Mary of Alpha and Omega and MY TWO LAWFUL BLACK BOYS MY LOVE.

JOHN THE LAWGIVER & His Brother Prince Emanuel the World's Swiftest Clergyman if you please my LOVE. PSALMS NO. 2. MY DEAR MONARCH, My Love, will you Darling, be PLEASED to have (all) My Love-Letters, Business & OTHER OFFICIAL DOCUMENTS, (Set-up) in SOLID WORK in EIGHT POINT TYPES.

AND I WILL PLACE them in my PSALMS MAKING DEPARTMENT AGAIN FOR YOU THE NEW BIBLE LAND (APRIL 27,1926) A.D. 2000.

CHAPTER 42
The Head Biblical Interpreter, Of Creation

The American "Rapers" Klu-Kluk-Klan and "Mob-Lynching Policy."

The (interpretation) these unfortunate ones, are the Outcome of the "Advance-Rate" on the Anglo-Saxon Slave Train.

"The ADVANCE-RATE" means, in time of Slavery, The WhiteSlave Masters, committed BOISTEROUS FORNICATION with THE BLACK WOMEN that were TAKEN for Slaves.

In those Days, THE BLACK MEN had no opportunity to (RATE) that is to Lie with Whitewomen.

Therefore, while the BLACK MEN'S BLOOD was BURNING UP IN THEIR bodies for the Sexual support of their OWN WOMEN, the WhiteSlave Masters TOOK away all the BEST BLACK WOMEN, and COMMITTED

Boisterous Fornication with them. And called it the Advance-Rate.

That is how the 3rd Class peoples come in to the human Veins.

IN THOSE DAYS this Act was called THE Advance-Rate of Whitesupremacy.

It is the UNIVERSAL SPIRIT OF ABUSE that manifest ITSELF that the Common-Class Black MEN are NOW Raping the common-Class Whitewomen.

Both rapers, Mob-Lynchers, and Klu-Kluk-Klangs are to be SHOT down from off the Face of GOD Almighty's Beautiful Earth.

His & Her Biblical Copyright, His & Her Majesty Queen Lula May Fitz Balintine Pettersburg, Head Biblical Interpreter of Creation.

CHAPTER 43

The Man Before Adam Was

I am His Majesty King Alpha The King of Kings, alone with my Own BONA FIDE Lion-Hearted Wife Queen Omega, THE BIBLICAL SOVEREIGN OF THIS WORLD.

We are Black Peoples if you please.

The Copyright of this World if you Please!!.

Race & Nations, Languages & Tongues & other peoples, will come and go, from off the FACE of this EARTH BUT His Majesty King Alpha and His Wife Queen Omega, We be here always if you please.

Alpha & Omega, The Black man & his wife, was here on Earth before Adam and Eve & ABARAHAM & Anglo-Saxon if you please.

And we, that is Our SEEDS will be here, in gross PROSPERITY as SOON AS THE ANGLO-SAXON PEOPLES ALL DIE OUT IF YOU PLEASE.

We are the Type-Setters for Time and Eternity, if you please. Our appointment is an Eternal Appointment if you please. We are, THE Keeper of the Tree of Life if you please.

We are the Owner of the Zodiac if you please.

We are The Ethiopian Kingdom Owner if you please.

We are His & Her Register General of Black Supremacy if you please.

Adam-Abraham-Angle-Saxon The Lepor, has no PLACE in this World, if you please.

Sign The Copyright of Creation. The Monarch F.B. Pettersburg A.B.C., M.A.

CHAPTER 44

My Royal Mother

My Mother Mrs. Ellen (Park) Johnson of Pettersburg, is my Virgin Mother; "this is to-day ....

She is that Royal Woman, that Landed me, The Monarch of Creation, on the SOIL of the Worlds Capital, Mt. Africa The Isles of Radiant Spring, the Triumphant Lot the New BIBLE Land.

Gross CREDIT IS DUE to the Black Peoples for such an indomitable Supreme drive.

Run to the Head of the World and STOP THE GIRL that can do IT right, and drench HER from the Eternal Power-House of Human Gravity.

I GUARANTEE This WORLD, that My Wife, Lady Pettersburg, will Land greater Men and Women than My Mother.

Because she has gotten a FIERCER DRENCH and a Rapider POWER on the Wheel of Time.

I have Just given my wife a FURIOUS Drench of BOISTEROUS RAGING Life: because we are the Equinoctial Equinox.

This Drench is called Genealogical Bottom.

HIS & HER COPYRIGHT MOTHER-HOOD the Monarch Fitz Balintine Pettersburg King of Kings.

BRIDEL YOUR CHILDREN BEFORE YOU ARE MARRIED.

CHAPTER 45

The Founder's Support Funds

The Register General office of Terrestrial Bequest.

K.A.Q.O.K.O.K.A.B.C.S.J.W.

His & Her Terrestrial Bequest Queen Lula May Fitz Balintine Pettersburg, Owner of the Holy Terrestrial Bar (Wills) & all Legal Bequests. A.B.C.K.A.D.O.K.O.K.S.G.C., Ph.D.,L.L.D.,S.J.W.C.D. P.M.O.H.T. K.O.T.T.L. Phol.C.L.C.

The Registered General Law Courts of Black Supremacy. The Church Triumphant, K.A.Q.O.K.O.K.A.B.C.,S.J.W.,Ph.D.,L.L.D., S.G.C.P.G.P.—M.O.H.T. Copyright, Lawgiver, Clergyman.

By His & Her Arch Monarch of Holy Time, Queen Lula May Fitz Balintine Pettersburg Equinoctial Equinox, S.J.W., K.A.Q.O.K.O.K.A.B.C. HEAD OF THIS WORLD & OWNER of MONEY MINT, HOLY THEOCRACY COMMUNICATION and DREAD LEXIUM(LEXICON) the FIRST & THE LAST.

THE REGISTERED GENERAL DEPARTMENT OF THE FOUNDER'S SUPPORT FUND K.O.K.

It is just, that Black Supremacy The Church Triumphant SUPPORT. The Foundationer from each Department, Whenever possible, His & Her Foundationer Queen Lula May Fitz Balintine Pettersburg, K.A.Q.O.

CHAPTER 46
Registered Library

Librarian's Register General Office of Black Supremacy, A.B.C.S.J.W.

Our Creative Sovereign of Mortal Libraries of Holy Time, The Lion & His Lioness of Alpha and Omega Queen Lula May Fitz BALINTINE PETTERSBURG OWNER OF MORTAL LIBRARIES BLACK FOLKS. The Royal Head oh the Church Triumphant, & The Eternal Angelic Hosts.

The Register General's Office of Communication by Black Supremacy the Great Triumphant Church K.A.Q.O.K.O.K., A.B.C.,S.J.W.,S.G.C. P.M.O.H.T.K.O.,T.T.L.C.L.C.

The Registered Business & Authorityship, of Black Supremacy.

This instrument protect the two sides of Authorityship, height and depth. The preference is always thrown over to the Church Triumphant. K.A.Q.O.S.J.W.K.O.K.

The Denouncement of the Militant Bible-Lands and Militant Dynasty. Any one found with any History, Record, or Books, or Bible from ADAM to Anglo-Saxon is guilty of Leze-Majesty, and is DEALT WITH AS SUCH. By the Dread order of the Church Triumphant. ETERNAL AFFIDAVIT.

The Register General Office, of The Triumphant Dynasty Great Black Supremacy.

By His & Her copyright Queen Lula May Fitz Balintine Pettersburg Owner of the Triumphant Dynasty & Great Black Supremacy. K.A.Q.O.K., O.K.C.L.C.

CHAPTER 47
The African Question

The African Question is this, The Continent of Africa Proper is a National Woman.

She is that Rich National Woman that has Charmed the Men of Nations to Lie With Her.

AND AFTER A TIME WHEN THEY ALL HAVE LIVED AND COHABITED WITH HER THEY ALL BROKE HER DOWN & LEAVE HER & PERSECUTE HER.

That is just how all Nations manage to SOKE through the AFRICAN WOMANHOOD of Prosperity.

She had too much Sympathy for the perishing Nations, whose Lives are Riotously Lived until this day.

SLAVE TRADERS WENT INTO AFRICA AND DAMAGED her Seeds, beyond any EARTHLY CURE.

BECAUSE SHE HAD TOO MUCH SYMPATHY FOR WILFULL IDLERS of Various Nations. SO THEY WENT INTO HER AND ROBBED her Lands, Money, and took her seeds, to be slaves.

That to-day she and her children have no Power in Her own Land, nor ABROAD.

AFRICAN CIVILIZATION.

All the African is to do now, Build a New.

Get out a New Dictionary & a New Bible & a New Board of Education, & a New Money Mint.

AND THE NEW OUTFIT SHALL BE CALLED BLACK SUPREMACY.

Signed by His & Her Majesty Queen Lula May Fitz Balintine Pettersburg HEAD OF THIS WORLD.

CHAPTER 47 A.

Atlas Survayor

Owing to the long Delay, of my BIBLE ATLAS SURVAYOR, and other DIFFICULTIES with the Engraving Department on this side of the Globe!!!

I had to alter the ENTIRE CONSTRUCTION of the CANON. Therefore 70, Seventy chapters are left out of this Volume.

Those you will get in One Full volume, as soon as Our Survayor & Atlas Engravers, can get through their work.

Has the Royal Honour to be, your Biblical Architect. His & Her ARCHITECT Queen Lula May Fitz Balintine Pettersburg, A.B.C., S.J.W.K.O.K.A.Q.O. ATLAS SURVAYORS. June 1st 1926. ETHIOPIAN BIBLE PIONEER.

P.S.—The entire Bible Scroll of Black Supremacy The Church Triumphant—and all the ROYAL DOCUMENTS Along with 76 chapters of The New Canon was destroyed by a MAD BRAINED REVIVAL man CALLED ALEXANDER HABAKKUK COOMBS and his Wife.

It is impossible for such a man to ESCAPE punishment because his acts are WILFULL.

The Rev. Fitz Balintine Pettersburg (Lawgiver) and Clergyman.

CHAPTER 48
The Map-Making and Bible Atlas Survayor

Owing to The Militant Objections to the Rise of the Church Triumphant, We had to have DETAINED Map-Making & Atlas Work, for much important Reasons.

The ENGRAVING Department, and The Atlas & Map-Making Philosopher, had much diffuculties with the Militant Power in the New Bible Land.

I, being The Triumphant Architect of the Church Triumphant I had UNTOLD Difficulties with the GENERATION of the 20th Century.

They were all, being Stung with the Sting of Death & SHAME and were not ABLE to APPRECIATE THE POWER OF LIFE.

Several groups of Books have been destroyed by the Militant Dread-nought in Different Continents of the Globe.

A great deal of Money has been lost, by TRUSTING it into the Hands of dishonest peoples.

THIS CODE is CALLED The Register Office of Black Supremacy.

Educated Men of ALL SHADES of Learning, are WANTED with money and without money. The same is applied to Women and Young people.

THE VEHEMENT VENERABLE FITZ BALINTINE PETTERSBURG REGISTER GENERAL of BLACK SUPREMACY. K.A.Q.O.K. O.K.S.J.W.A.B.C., L.L.D.

CHAPTER 48A
Owner of the Zodiac

THE REGISTER GENERAL OFFICE OF ASTROLOGY, BY THE KING OF KINGS, OWNER OF THE ZODIAC.

His & Her Monarch of Renown Queen Lula May Fitz Balintine Pettersburg King of Kings, Equinoctial Equinox, Head of This World, Owner of the Zodiac, K.A.Q.,O.K.O.K.,Ph.D., L.L.D., A.B.C.S.J.W.P.M.H.T.K.O.T T.O.L. P.C.C.L.

All Astrologers by Compulsory Must be Registered at the Register Office of Astrology, by order of the Owner of the Zodiac.

Astrologers are all guilty of the Crime of Genealogical, Sexual, Mortal Suicide. They have read the Signs of The Zodiac to suite Whitesupremacy, the Grand Whore of this World.

They have Transfigured the Adamic-Serpent into a tip-top Astrological Master Scorpion and planted the Beast right into the ROOT of the PRIVATE OF THE ZODIAC.

We The Head of This Earth and Other Worlds, are not (responsible) for Astrological Stupidity and WhiteRulers ignorance.

God Almighty is INSULTED by ASTROLOGERS.

Also all soundly thinking Human Beings on the Train of Time.

CHAPTER 49

Psalm 50 By the Monarch Pettersburg

Psalms are the Music of the TREE of life.

THE TREE of the Zodiac was much DISHONOURED by Angle-MILITANT Astrologers.

His & Her Supreme Registered crown Manuscript of the Great Zodiac of His Majesty King Alpha and his Wife, Queen Omega, the Lion and his Lioness, Pettersburg and His Wife Lula; Owner of the Canopy.

Their Superior Registered Manuscript of all Angle-Militant Works.

Planted a CROWNED CAPITAL of MOST HOLY CREATION, CALLED MT. AFRICA.

THE CANOPY OF THE MOST HOLY & LIVING GOD OF BOISTEROUS LOVE.

Deeper and Sounder than the Anglo-Saxon (Slave) Manuscript at the Monistry of St. Augustine at English Canterbury, since A.D. 1000.

SWEET HEART, GREAT BLACK SUPREMACY YOUR TRUE LOVER TOOK DOWN The Angle-Militant Slaves, The Twentieth Century, A.D. 2000.

I am the Supreme Judge of Holy Time, Angle-Militant Crime Against the TRUE and Most Holy Creator, is Eternal Leze Majesty.

MY SON, THE PSALMIST DAVID ASK ME TO CLOSE UP THE PIT FOR HIM.

I am YOUR Vehement Venerable Psalmist and Bible Editor of the 'TREE of Life, PETTERSBURG THE MONARCH of Creation (from the Throne) June 2, 1926.

CHAPTER 50
The Theological Lawgiver Of Creation

To THE BAR OF MOST HOLY THEOLOGY.

MY DEAR THEOLOGY, I AM YOUR PAST EXCEEDING DREAD CREATOR AND BIBLICAL SOVEREIGN.

I am the Man before Adam and Eve and Abraham the Anglo-Saxon.

I am His Arch Sovereign of Most Holy Time, King Alpha, the King of Kings. My wife, your Arch Sovereign Queen Omega, Her Tri-Virginity and Myself His Tri-Divinity, We have given Our Names according to Bible Law.

FROM THE NEW TESTAMENT CODE, The Revelation of John the Divine.

We came down on the Anglo-Saxon Slave Train, in order that we could get to have crossed the Militant Gulf at the Gate-way of Nationality.

Now nations time is up, for National Rulership, they must give way to the POWER HOUSE of THE Great Black Supremacy. The Church Triumphant.

Therefore, all Theological PLANTS, must be RENOVATED, TO BE ABLE TO FACE THE VULCAN of The Church Triumphant.

Theology, my love, call or WRITE to the p. 83 Registered Office of Holy Theology at the World's Capital for your New THEOLOGICAL Diploma.

His and Her Arch-Groom and Bride Queen Lula May Fitz Balintine Pettersburg: Biblical-Arch-Sovereign, Equinoctial Equinox, Owner of the Zodiac and communication.

Black Supremacy Perfect Parchment Scroll, Holy Theocracy Most Dread Copy number 5 K.A.Q.O.K.O.K.

This Powerful Canon is the Narrative of His and Her Dynasty Queen Lula May Fitz Balintine Pettersburg, A,.B.C.S.J.W. KING OF KINGS.

We are not RELATED to Militant Genesis Pentatouch, Apocrypha, Romanic or Scientific, Blue-Murder.

The Perfect Diploma. Number ONE IS OUR LIVE LINE TWIXT TIME AND ETERNITY: ETHIOPIAN PARCHMENT SCROLL.

1. Diploma

The Bible Owner is THE Black Man.

The Bible's Supreme Name is Holy Theocracy and Lady Diety, Creation's SUPREMACY.

Copyright of Creation, Creator of Dynasties and Governments, Marriage officer, Supreme Judge, Lawgiver, and Paymaster of Holy Time.

Pen and Power Master and Founder of Holy p. 84 Communication and Owner of the Human Family.

The Monarch Finger on the Right Limb, is Holy Union's Perfect finger.

"MY Diploma," is The Human Race, Theocracy, and Dictionary in One.

The Twelve months of the year are my (12) Degrees, "Celestial Diploma."

I am The Holy Bible's Owner, therefore, I have taken away the Adamic, imperfect (version) that is (dated) B.C. 4004 and closed A.D. 96.

And give to Creation, my perfect Husband and Wife's Theocracy (dated) A.D. 1925 AND 26.

Clear God the Father's Perfect Reputation and The Tree of Life.

Equinoctial Equinox.

To Her Arch Majesty, the Lioness, Her Ethiopian Tri-Virginity, of Alpha and Omega Queen Lula May Fitz Balintine Pettersburg Equinoctial Equinox, K.A.Q.O. My Equator.

My dear Wife, I am your Husband King Alpha the Lion of Man.

December 1st 1925 A.D. I gave to His Majesty the Great Hector Joseph My chief Copyright Attorney at "The world's

Capital" Our Matrimonial Affadavit, K.A.Q.O. The Virgin, Equinoctial Equinox.

Now my Dear Honourable Virgin, Your Arch Majesty, Mrs. Lula May Fitz Balintine Pettersburg Equinoctial Equinox.

Now Sweet Heart, my dear wonder, just take this Drench of Perfect Wonders and Live with me for Life.

We being the Keeper of the TREE OF LIFE.

The Terrestrial Guest Chamber.

Now Dear Heart, before we take charge of the Guest Chamber of Creation, we have to clear God the Father's Perfect Reputation and the Tree of Life.

We being the Keeper of the TREE of Life, we are requested to call up the Mental Power House of this world, and have THEIR BEST Physician to (Loose) YOUR Virgin matrix and give us a crown Diploma of our Dignity.

December 27 1925 A.D. From the Judgment Throne by the King of Kings.

A.B.C.K.A.Q.O.K.O.K.C.L.C.S.J.W.Ph.D.L.L.D.,P.M .O.H.T.

The Chief Virgin of the Tree of Life, By Order of the Copyright of Creation.

To Creation Vast the Medical Board of creation.

His and Her Majesty King Alpha and Queen Omega Medical Practitioners, s.s.s.s., December 27 1925, 9 O.C. A.M. A.D. 2000. World's Capital.

Perfect law.—the Holy Physician. My Dear Perfect Physician, you are (Requested) by His and Her Ethiopian

Triumphant Dynasty (To Loose) the Virgin Matri Her Tri-Virginity Her Ethiopian Triumphant Dynasty, Queen Lula May Fitz Balintine Pettersburg before she enter Her Husband's Guest Chamber.

The Copyright Department of Holy Time and give to the Perfect Bar of Holy Theocracy this World's Medical Affidavit.

The most Holy Ground of Perfect Living Truth, also His Tri-Divinity.

By His and Her Dynasty, the Tri-Monarch, Lady, Lula May Fitz Balintine Pettersburg, copyright Philosopher, Physician, Clergyman and Lawgiver. S.S.S.S. ETHIOPIA'S DYNASTY DIPLOMA, ORDINATION, PROCLAMATION AND ROYAL DOCUMENT.

His and Her Arch-Sovereign King Alpha and Queen Omega Supreme Crown Lawgiver.

Crown DOCUMENT. The Royal name of this ETHIOPIAN DYNASTY is called "Black Supremacy" Denouncement. The Angle Saxon Slave Dynasty is called Whitesupremacy, Denounce him.

Official Order. By the Sacred Order of His Majesty, Our Live Creator the Living God, Heaven and Earth Superior.

Black. Supremacy starts December 23, 7 O.C.P.M. A.D. 1925. We Cross Whitesupremacy that Sacred Hour for Eternal Life.

And take off the Black man from off the Anglo-Saxon Slave Train that Hour.

Christianity and Civilisation is now Black Supremacy.
NAME
CONTINENT
ADDRESS
BUSINESS

Biblical Interpretation

Introduction

Fitz Balintine Pettersburg begins with —"My dear inhabitants of this world, we are the foundation stones of the resurrection of the Kingdom of Ethiopia." Pettersburg intended the Royal Parchment Scroll (RPS) to be read by a global Black audience. Once the knowledge contained herein was revealed the intended effect was the shifting change of the religious consciousness of a degraded and oppressed race. The RPS was meant as an alternative to the White theology forced upon people of African descent as a means to sever all historical, sociological and metaphysical connections to Africa. To counter the debilitating effects of White supremacy Pettersburg sought to redeem the Black nation by uplifting Black womanhood to an exalted status, reclaim Africa, destroy White supremacy and to uplift Black consciousness.

The reclamation of Black womanhood is central to the RPS. To reclaim Black national sovereignty meant the redemption of Black womanhood. Black women were they key to the suppression of the Black race therefore slave laws, particularly those in the Americas mandated that Negro women's children to serve according to the condition of their mother. The American colony of Virginia was one of the first colonies to legislate the status of the child based on the status of the mother in 1662:

Act XII

Negro womens [sic] *children to serve according to the condition of the mother.*

WHEREAS some doubts have arrisen whether children got by any Englishman upon a Negro woman should be slave or free, Be it therefore enacted and declared by this present grand assembly, that all children borne in this country shalbe held bond or free only according to the condition of the mother, And that if any christian shall committ ffornication with a Negro man or woman, hee or shee soe offending shall pay double the ffines imposed by the former act. [1]

The raping, beating and degrading of Black women was psychological warfare meant as means to shame and degrade Black men. No redemption of Africa or the Black race was possible without the redemption of Black women and hence the uplift of Black men.

This text should be read as a statement of Black Diasporic

---

1. Act XII, *Laws of Virginia*, December 1662 (Hening, *Statutes at Large*, 2: 170). Taken from https://memory.loc.gov/ammem/awhhtml/awlaw3/slavery.html

Biblical Interpretation

nationalism, a call for the unification of Black people through the re-aligning of Black religiosity toward Ethiopia. In short, Pettersburgs' goal is to provide a religious text that will liberate the minds of the Black people so that there may come a spiritual unification of Blacks around a theocratic and afrocentric national identity.

The socio-religious centering of the Black nation is the basis by which Pettersburg and other religious, cultural and political leaders and organizations of the 19th and the early 20th century were almost universally aligned. The redemption of or praise of all things African sometimes referred to as "Ethiopianism," was central to giving the race an unequivocal reprieve from centuries of psychological damage to the prestige of Africa.

Ethiopia's symbolic imagery was intertwined with Black Christian theology, as expressed in Psalm 68:31: "Princes shall come out of Egypt, Ethiopia shall soon stretch forth her hands unto God." An appreciation of the power of Ethiopianism, as a shaping force, is essential to understanding Black intellectual thought of the 19th century, and summarily its influence on 20th-century Black liberation theology. A close reading of the introduction of the RPS reveals the rising of consciousness of Blacks within the Diaspora and the centering of Ethiopia as the resurrected Kingdom of God.

The foundation of any religious belief has to begin with the acknowledgement of a supreme power, deity or life force that has, in some mysterious way brought forth life from and into the vast empty reaches of the cosmos. Pettersburg wrote "My dear inhabitants of this world, we are the foundation stones of the resurrection of the Kingdom of Ethiopia." Pettersburg is firm in his claim that people of African descent are in fact the bedrock upon which the walls of the Kingdom of Ethiopia are to be built.

Nothing did more to consciously shape Ethiopianism than did the invasion of the Empire of Ethiopia by the Kingdom of Italy in 1896. The Kingdom of Italy's quest to better its position in Africa by seizing Ethiopia proved to be a critical moment in the search by Africans to not only liberate themselves from European domination but to vindicate African manhood. King Menelik II, Negus of Ethiopia and his army decisively destroyed the invading Italian force at the Battle of Adwa (1896) (The same year of Plessy v. Ferguson). The Italian Kingdom suffered such horrendous losses that news of the defeat emboldened Blacks worldwide.

The Ethiopian or Abyssinian Empire was located in the region of what is the modern nation of Ethiopia. Its existence spans from 1137 AD to 1974 AD. The history of the Ethiopian dynasty must be considered as integral to the rise of the world's great Abrahamic religions. The Solomonic dynasty, also known as the House of Solomon, is the former ruling Imperial House of the Ethiopian Empire. Its members claim patrilineal descent from King Solomon of Israel and the Queen of Sheba. Tradition asserts that the Queen gave birth to Menelik I after her biblically described visit to Solomon in Jerusalem. Menelik I is the first Solomonic Emperor of Ethiopia, and the son of King Solomon of ancient Israel and Makeda (Queen of Sheba). Menelik I ruled circa 950 BC. Religious tradition credits him with bringing the Ark of the Covenant to Ethiopia, following a visit to Jerusalem to meet his father Solomon upon reaching adulthood.

According to the Kebra Nagast[2] King Solomon had intended on sending one son of each of his nobles and one son of each temple priest with Menelik I upon his return to his mother's kingdom. He had a replica made of the Ark for them to take with them. Upon the death of Queen Makeda, Menelik I assumed the throne with the new title of Emperor and *King of Kings of Ethiopia*. Menelik I founded the Solomonic dynasty of Ethiopia that ruled Ethiopia with few interruptions for close to three thousand years (225 generations ended with the fall of Emperor Haile Selassie I in 1974).[3]

---

2. The *Kebra Nagast* or *The Glory of the Kings* is a 14th-century account written in Ge'ez of the origins of the Solomonic line of the Emperors of Ethiopia. The text, in its existing form, is at least 700 years old and is considered by many Ethiopian Christians and Rastafari to be a historically reliable work.

3. A counter argument has been raised that should be addressed. This line of argument asserts that kings of Ethiopia are only witnessed in the record from the 8th century BC when there was a kingdom named D'mt located in Eritrea and northern Ethiopia that existed during the late 8th to 5th centuries BC. Few inscriptions by or about this kingdom exist. As a result, it is not known whether D'mt ended as a civilization before the Kingdom of Axum was established on the Red Sea coast in the 5th century BC, evolved into the Aksumite state, or was one of the smaller states united in the Aksumite kingdom possibly around the beginning of the 1st century AD.

It is worth highlighting the quote in its entirety from the Kebra Negast because of the power of evoking the direct link between the Kingdom of Ethiopia and the Solomonic dynasty and hence the Kingdom of God:

> *"And when the young man arrived in his mother's country he rejoiced there in the honour [which he received], and in the gifts [that were made] to him. And when the people saw him they thought him to be the perfect likeness of SOLOMON the King. And they made obeisance to him, and they said unto him, "Hail, the royal father liveth!" And they brought unto him gifts and offerings, fatted cattle and food, as to their king. And [the people of] the whole country of GÂZÂ, as far as the border of JUDAH, were stirred up and they said, "This is King SOLOMON." And there were some who said, "The King is in JERUSALEM building his house"—now he had finished building the House of God—and others said, "This is SOLOMON the King, the son of DAVID." And they were perplexed, and they disputed with one another, and they sent off spies mounted on horses, who were to seek out King SOLOMON and to find out if he were actually in JERUSALEM, or if he were with them [in GÂZÂ]. And the spies came to the watchmen of the city of JERUSALEM, and they found King SOLOMON there, and they made obeisance to him, and they said unto him, "Hail, may the royal father live! [Our] country is disturbed because there*

hath come into it a merchant who resembleth thee in form and appearance, without the smallest alteration or variation. He resembleth thee in noble carriage and in splendid form, and in stature and in goodly appearance; he lacketh nothing in respect of these and is in no way different from thyself. His eyes are gladsome, like unto those of a man who hath drunk wine, his legs are graceful and slender, and the tower of his neck is like unto the tower of DAVID thy father. He is like unto thee exactly in every respect, and every member of his whole body is like unto thine."

And King SOLOMON answered and said unto them, "Where is it then that he wisheth to go?" And they answered and said unto him, "We have not enquired of him, for he is awesome like thyself. But his own people, when we asked them, 'Whence have ye come and whither do ye go?' said, 'We have come from the dominions of HENDAKÊ (CANDACE) and ETHIOPIA, and we are going to the country of JUDAH to King SOLOMON.'" And when King SOLOMON heard this his heart was perturbed and he was glad in his soul, for in those days he had no children, except a boy who was seven years old and whose name was ÎYÔRBE'ÂM (REHOBOAM). It happened to SOLOMON even as Paul stateth, saying, "God hath made foolishness the wisdom of this world,"[1] for SOLOMON had made a plan in his wisdom and said, "By one thousand women I shall beget one thousand men children, and I shall inherit the countries of the enemy, and I will overthrow [their] idols." But [God] only gave him three children. His eldest son was the King of ETHIOPIA, the son of the Queen of ETHIOPIA, and was the firstborn of whom [God] spake prophetically, "God sware unto DAVID in righteousness, and repented not, 'Of the fruit of thy body will I make to sit upon thy throne.'" And God gave unto DAVID His servant grace before Him, and granted unto him that there should sit upon the throne of Godhead One of his seed in the flesh, from the Virgin, and should judge the living and the dead, and reward every man according to his work, One to whom praise is meet, our Lord JESUS CHRIST, for ever and ever, Amen. And He gave him one on the earth who should become king over the Tabernacle of the Law of the holy, heavenly ZION, that is to say, the King of ETHIOPIA. And as for those who reigned, who were not [of] ISRAEL, that was due to the transgression of the law and the commandment, whereat God was not pleased."[4]

The sacred image of Menelik II, baptized as Sahle Maryam (1844 – 1913) was instrumental in the role of shaping modern Black religious consciousness throughout the Diaspora. Ethiopia derived prestige for having shown the world that an African–Black army could defeat a European

---

4. The *Kebra Negast*: 34. "*How the young man arrived in his mother's country.*"

power on its terms. However, Italian Fascist Benito Mussolini reasserted European expansionist claims, culminating in the Italian occupation of Ethiopia in October 1935. The Italian occupation of Ethiopia would end with the Allied Forces victory in World War II and the coronation of His Imperial Majesty (H.I.M) Haile Selassie I as Emperor.

One of the most prophetic aspects of the RPS is its foretelling of the reemergence of the Ethiopian Empire. At the time of the writing of the RPS Ras Tafari (Haile Selassie I) had toured the Middle East and Europe visiting most of the major European capitals and historic Middle Eastern cities. News of Ras Tafari and his regally dressed entourage both stunned and marveled the host populations. The New York Times carried the story with the headlines, "Ethiopian Ruler Wins Paludits of Parisians: Ras Taffari's [sic] Oriental Dignity Impresses Poulace-Governments Extends Royal Honors." The New York Times recognized the claims of Ras Tafari as the rightful heir to the throne of Menelik by referring to him as "the descendant of King Solomon." The entourage was described at "gorgeously robed Ethiopian Kings." Ras Tafari presented lions to French Prime Minister Raymond Poincare and United Kingdom's King George V. Global accounts of Ras Tafari's imperial promise spread as he ceremoniously displayed an air of dignity that conferred his status as, while not materially as prosperous as some European heads of State he was, in terms of history, first among equals.

Pettersburg reminds those seeking the resurrection of Ethiopia that a Covenant with God must be established and fulfilled by the people. The religious or spiritual binding of people has long been a primary act in yoking people to a set of spiritual doctrines. By working for the redemption of Ethiopia would signal a fulfillment of this Covenant. The establishment of a duty to prepare the way for the rising of the Ethiopian Kingdom would, in fact, establish the basis for the idea of Blacks not simply as a covenanted people but as a *chosen people.*

The 1920s were a remarkable period in world economic history. The world's industrial power was harnessed to its full destructive power during the First World War. The mass commercialization and hyper industrialization of the world's economies were well underway with the onset of 20th-century global capitalism. Those nations that were capable of harnessing the earth's productive and destructive forces would be at a greater advantage. Knowledge was increasingly becoming a premium commodity in the post first world war industrial world. Pettersburg stressed the importance of knowledge as the basis by which the new Kingdom will arise by writing, "In my Encyclopedia I will explain to you all, how worlds are being built and what triggers Kingdoms are set on." The use of an encyclopedia as a source of knowledge had come into prominence in the 1920s. Harmsworth's Universal Encyclopedia and the Children's Encyclopedia appeared in the early 1920s and for most families that could afford popular encyclopedias such as World Book. These books became necessary household items in the early 1920s.

Pettersburg made knowledge necessary for the redemption of the Africa and its people. He wrote, "I hand you my Rule Book from the poles of Supreme Authority." Leonard Howell acknowledged the Rule Book as a necessity for Ethiopia's redemption. Howell wrote, "Speaking for the Universe and the womanhood of man Queen Omega the Ethiopian woman is the crown woman of this world. She hands us Her Rule-Book from the poles of supreme authority she is the Cannon Mistress of creation." The Rule Book's importance is that it was intended to lead us to various departments and regulations of the Kingdom. It was intended that these regulations would guide Blacks toward ethical religious behavior and ultimately become the basis of the re-emerged Kingdom.

Pettersburg signed the end of this section with "I am the Canon Mistress of Creation. Kingston Jamaica, B.W.I. Tropic of Cancer." The idea of a mistress of creation is typical of the world's creation mythologies. The Tropic of Cancer, is also referred to as the Northern Tropic, is currently 23°26'13.2" (or 23.43699°) north of the Equator. It is the most northerly circle of latitude on earth at which the sun can be directly overhead. Its Southern Hemisphere counterpart, marking the most southerly position at which the Sun can be directly overhead, is the Tropic of Capricorn. These tropics are two of the five major circles of latitude that mark maps of Earth. The positions of these two circles of latitude (relative to the Equator) are dictated by the tilt of Earth's axis of rotation relative to the plane of its orbit. The distance between the Tropic of Cancer and Jamaica is approximately three hundred and seventy-six miles or six hundred six kilometers.

Ethiopia's Preface

Pettersburg presents the idea of the Rule Book standing as the road junction from which signs project in the direction of the place or route into the Kingdom of Ethiopia. At the time of the writing, the United Kingdom and other European nation states had so thoroughly colonized much of the Black world it would have seemed to Pettersburg and his contemporaries that the Anglo (Angle) Saxon world had laid over the earth a veil of White supremacy.

The four points of the globe correspond to the four corners of the cosmos. These four points are called the four magnetic poles of the globe. In astronomical science, this also corresponds to the galactic quadrant, or quadrant of the Galaxy, as one of four circular sectors in the division of the Milky Way Galaxy. In actual astronomical practice, the delineation of the galactic quadrants is based upon the galactic coordinate system, which places the Sun as the pole or center of the mapping system. Ethiopia is, like the Sun, the axis mundi or navel of the world. The number four is synonymous of Matthew, Mark, Luke, and John and symbolic of the four faces of Yeshua (King, Ox, Man, Eagle) and the four horns of the altar.[5]

Two aspects of the document that are intriguing is the insistence on academic decorum and the consistent inclusion of Queen Lula. Pettersburg signed this section of the document "His & Her Dynasty Queen Lula may Fitz Balintine Pettersburg, S.J.W., A B.C. Ph.D., L.L.,K.O.K." (Titles were meant to signify competency). For much of Black life in the America's education mattered for Black people so much so that Marcus Garvey stressed that knowledge was a fundamental aspect of becoming a well-respected and prosperous citizen of the world. The addition of Queen Lula certainly places women as a dynamic force within the plan of the RPS. In the introduction, Pettersburg stated, "Speaking for the Universe, and the Womanhood of Man, I the Ethiopian woman, is the Crown woman of the world." Relate this to Revelation 12:1 that states: *A great sign appeared in heaven: a woman clothed with the sun, with the moon under her feet and a crown of twelve stars on her head. She was pregnant and cried out in pain as she was about to give birth.*[6] According to Genesis 37:9,10, these represented the first family of Israel: Jacob (the "sun"), Rachel (the "moon"), and Jacob's twelve sons (the "twelve stars"). Israel was the "embodiment" the

---

5. Allison Brown, *The End...Prophetic Insights into the Last Days* (Lulu.com), 242.
6. The woman clothed with the sun and moon under her feet symbolizes God's people in the Old and the New Testament. Israel of old gave birth to the Messiah and then became the new Israel, the Church.

Torah or Law, which is God's eternal commandments, rules, and guidelines.[7]

Ethiopia's Fly Leaf

The reference to a fly leaf can symbolize a blank page at the beginning or end of a book or document. This most likely refers to a new dawn, symbolized by a blank page that can be written by the people of Ethiopia.

While there is no way to pinpoint Pettersburg thoughts here we do know that this time period ushered in air flight as an emerging mode of transportation early 20th century. The 1920s were an important decade for air travel. The Holy Piby as well as the RPS hint to the emergence of this new technology. Aircraft became a common sight as advancements in technology took off between World War I (1914 – 1918) and World War II (1939 – 1945). Airplanes evolved from biplanes made from wood and fabric to sleek, high-powered aluminum monoplanes. After World War I experienced pilots became barnstormers, flying into small towns and taking anyone that could afford to pay for a ride at an air show.

The creation of national air service and launches from sea carriers were all instrumental in pushing advances in aviation. Pettersburg noted, "*I am going to teach the Princess to fly around the poles.*" There are many Biblical symbols of flight—Isaiah 40:31: "*but those who wait for the Lord shall

---

7. http://www.tedmontgomery.com/bblovrvw/emails/thewoman.html.

renew their strength, they shall mount up with wings like eagles, they shall run and not be weary, they shall walk and not faint." Psalm 104:3-4 : *"you set the beams of your chambers on the waters, you make the clouds your chariot, you ride on the wings of the wind, you make the winds your messengers, fire and flame your ministers."*

CHAPTER 1

The Ethiopian Western Philosophy

Trees are one of the worlds most ancient and important religious symbols. The symbol of the Cosmic Tree has been projected by the psyche of variety of the world's people who the tree as a primary element in their religious systems.[8] Trees symbolize the cosmic development in death and regeneration. Further, the imagery of roots extending deeply into the soil and its branches reaching upward is universally regarded as the connection between heaven and Earth. Rastafari are deeply conscious of "roots" bringing forth the tree that then brings forth fruit of knowledge for human consumption. Getting to the "Roots" is essential for recognizing one's eternal being (*atman*).

The "supreme Book of Royal Rules from the Ethiopian Western Repository" might suggest that the creation of a

---

8. Jean Chevalier and Alain Gheerbrant, *Dictionary of Symbols* (New York: Penguin Books, 1996), 1027.

Biblical Interpretation

journal where some form of rules would be kept. Ethiopian Repository might, in fact, allude to *The African Repository* that was published in the late 19th century in Washington DC. This volume was published by *The Society for the Colonization of Free People of Color of America*, commonly known as the American Colonization Society (ACS). Robert Finely of New Jersey established the ACS in 1816. The ACS supported the migration of free African Americans to Africa and helped found the colony of Liberia in 1821–22 as a colony for free American Blacks slaves.

Illustration

To Rend means to tear or wrench violently or to cause great emotional pain. Here we see a reminder of the destruction of Ancient Kingdoms and the spreading of its people into Bands or groups of people that have come to populate the world. This would apply to Blacks are part of a larger Diaspora.

Pettersburg declares that he is the Blaming Mistress of many worlds. Balm Yards were traditionally known as provincial or local hospitals run mostly by people experience in traditional healing. Healing is an important aspect of Rastafari biblical texts. See Chapter Two, Royal Move.

The Rule Book

The repetitive imagery of the Rule Book as we saw in the RPS Introduction. The Rule Book is necessary because it was intended to lead us into different departments of the Kingdom and to the records of the Kingdom. It was intended by that these regulations would point toward the basis of the Kingdom. The Royal Angel Band represents the emerging Ethiopians.

The parable of Jesus and the Woman of Samaria is fascinating. It appears that Pettersburg uses the imagery of the unknown, nameless woman as an example of someone who initially refused the request of Christ because she was spiritually blind. Pettersburg wrote: "THE WELL OF SAMARIA.—the Woman at first refused to obey the request of Our Lord because she was spiritually blind.?"

What is also striking of this particular insertion of this parable is that the retreat of Jesus to Galilee through Samaria, has been described as the first turning point in his life. For one the Pharisees begin to see Jesus as a hostile intrusion. Jesus by resting at Jacob's well is a living symbol of the old patriarchal way of life and the emergence of a new evangelistic way. It represents the essence of Africans in the diaspora-Jesus' condescending pity on the Samarian woman and her subsequent conversion. How the grace of Christ can break through the Babylonian restrictions to a new light and spirit.[9]

Ancient Samaria was located in the Land of Israel, one of the three divided areas of the Holy Land in the time of

---

9. Johan Peter Lange, *A Commentary on the Holy Scriptures: Critical, Doctrinal and Homiletical, with Special References to Minsters and Students*, (New York: Charles Scribner's Sons, 1900), 168.

Christ, with Galilee to the north and Judea to the south, the Jordan to the east and the Mediterranean on the west. It was the capital of the northern Kingdom of Israel in the 9th and 8th centuries BC. Samaria occupied parts of the territory assigned at first to Ephraim, Mahasseh, and Issachar, Luke 17:11,[10] John 4:4.[11] John the Baptist's body is thought to be buried in Samaria. In 721 BCE Assyria conquered Israel and sent most of its people to live in Assyria. The Assyrians replaced the original people with five alien tribes who resettled the area (2 Kings 17:13-34). Christ came to Sychar, which was a town near Jacob's Well.

The Parable of Jesus and the woman of Samaria is covered in John 4: "A woman from Samaria came to draw water. Jesus said to her, 'Give me a drink.' (For his disciples had gone away into the city to buy food.) The Samaritan woman said to him, 'How is it that you, a Jew, ask for a drink from me, a woman of Samaria?' (For Jews have no dealings with Samaritans.) Jesus answered her, "If you knew the gift of God, and who it is that is saying to you, 'Give me a drink,' you would have asked him, and he would have given you living water." The Samaritan woman at the well is a figure from the Gospel of John, in John 4:4–26. In the traditions of the Eastern Orthodox Church, she is considered to be a saint, named Photine (the luminous one, from φως, "light"). We

---

10. The faith of Jesus manifested by the foreigner that has brought him salvation.
11. Geographically Jews often bypassed Samaria by taking a route across the Jordan.

should note here that Jesus has the longest conversation with any one person and this happens to be a non-Jewish woman.

The Dove is symbolic with that of the olive branch, and the story of Noah and the Flood. In Christian Iconography, a dove also symbolizes the Holy Spirit, in reference to Matthew 3:16[12] and Luke 3:22[13] where the Holy Spirit is compared to a dove at the Baptism of Jesus.[14] The dove acquired its present meaning among early Christians, and was confirmed by St Augustine of Hippo in his book *On Christian Doctrine*.

Pettersburg makes an analogy here that like Jesus who brought the woman to the recognition that he was the Messiah Pettersburg makes this connection to bring his people out of spiritual blindness as Jesus did with the Samaritan woman.

---

12. *"And when Jesus had been baptized, just as he came up from the water, suddenly the heavens were opened to him and he saw the Spirit of God descending like a dove and alighting on him."*
13. *"...and the Holy Spirit descended upon him in bodily form like a dove. And a voice came from heaven, "You are my Son, the Beloved; with you I am well pleased."*
14. The rock dove is, due to its relation to the homing pigeon and thus communications, the main image in the crest of the Tactical Communications Wing, a body within the Royal Air Force. Below the crest is the Wing's motto, "Ubique Loquimur" or "We Speak Everywhere."

CHAPTER 2
The Royal Move

Seven angels sound the seven trumpets and the events that follow are described in detail from Revelation Chapters 8 to 11. According to Revelation 8:1-2, the angels sound these trumpets after the breaking of the seventh seal. These seals secured the apocalyptic document that was in the right hand of *Him* who sits on the main throne.

The word "Bands" refers to associations of families living together. They are loosely allied by marriage, descent, friendship, and common interest. "Bands" have been found primarily among foragers, especially self-sufficient pedestrian foragers. The total number of people within these societies rarely exceeds a few dozen. The primary integrating mechanism for these societies is kinship. Bands are extremely egalitarian—all families are essentially equal. There is no economic class differentiation. However, there are, at times, clear status differences based on gender and age.[15]

---

15. http://anthro.palomar.edu/political/pol_2.htm.

Jesus did not practice baptism except for his disciples (John 3:22). The actual work of baptizing was left to his disciples. The imagery here is to connect with repentance, cleansing, and identification of the work that needs to be done.

We see again the imagery of Doves. Doves, usually White in color, are used in a variety of settings as symbols of love, peace or as messengers. Doves appear in the symbolism of Judaism, Christianity and Paganism, and of both military and pacifist groups. The use of a dove and olive branch as a symbol of peace originated with the early Christians, who portrayed the act of baptism accompanied by a dove holding an olive branch in its beak and also used the image on their sepulchers.

CHAPTER 3
The Healing Plough Of Creation

Chapter three presents the necessary spiritual guidance for the healing of righteous. Before any man/woman who stands in judgment she must be healed in order that she may have everlasting life. Revelations 22:2: *"through the middle of the street of the city. On either side of the river is the tree of life with its twelve kinds of fruit, producing its fruit each month; and the leaves of the tree are for the healing of the nations."*[16] Those standing before judgment must be healed from the effects of selfishness and man's inability to love his fellow man. Only through the healing of men, particularly the healing of Black men and women, after suffering from a world controlled by White supremacy will the generations of Blacks be able to enter into the Kingdom.

---

16. This is a reference to the tree in the primeval paradise (Gn. 2:9). The decree excluding humanity from the tree of life has been revoked by Christ.

Healing will take place in a Balm Yard. In Jamaica, a Balm Yard is traditionally known as a place where local healers would attend to the sick. In the Book of the *All-Virtuous Wisdom of Joshua ben Sira*, commonly called the Wisdom of Sirach or simply Sirach, and also known as the Book of Ecclesiasticus is a work of ethical teachings from approximately 200 to 175 BCE written by the Jewish scribe Shimon ben Yeshua ben Eliezer ben Sira of Jerusalem. In the book of Sira, Chapter 38 "Sickness and Death" verse 4 "God makes the earth yield healing herbs which the prudent should not neglect."[17] Those who have given themselves, body and soul to Jah and believe in the power of the living Jah will gain admission to the Balm Yard.

Healing comes from the servants of Jah (the consecrated men and women)— the Holy, who reigns over the nations as "servant kings" just as Yahshua was in His days on the earth. To serve Jah is to work toward a deep healing to the nations, to minister to those who have gone through the struggle, slavery, segregation, colonialism, hardship, pain, suffering, and finally death. In the eternal age, the people of the nations, as in this case the Black people of Jah, who have

---

17. Sirach is accepted as part of the Christian biblical canons by Catholics, Eastern Orthodox, and most of Oriental Orthodox. The Anglican Church does not accept Sirach as protocanonical, and say it should be read only "for example of life and instruction of manners; but yet doth not apply them to establish any doctrine." See "Canon VI. *Of the Sufficiency of the Holy Scriptures for salvation*. The Thirty-Nine Articles of Religion." Church Society. http://www.churchsociety.org/issues_new/doctrine/39a/iss_doctrine_39A_Arts06-08.asp

been granted a second life will need healing by the leaves of the Tree of Life, which will be administered the servants of Jah. Ganja or herb is the healing of the nation. Genesis 9:3 proclaims: "Everything that lives and moves about will be food for you. Just as I gave you the green plants, I now give you everything."

Pettersburg invokes the name of Melchizedek. Melchizedek is a king and priest appearing in the Book of Genesis. The name as interpreted means "King of Righteousness." In Hebrews 7: "This Melchizedek was King of Salem (Jerusalem) and priest of God Most High. "Salem" comes from the Hebrew word meaning "peace." That would make Melchizedek a king of peace. Melchizedek is the first individual to be given the title Kohen (priest) in the Hebrew Bible. In the King James Version, the Book of Psalms names Melchizedek as representative of the priestly line through which a future king of Israel's Davidic line was to be ordained. Melchizedek met Abraham returning from the defeat of the kings and he blessed him. Abraham gave him a tenth of everything.[18]

Melchizedek is referred to again in Hebrews 5:6-10; Hebrews 6:20; Hebrews 7:1-21: "Thou art a priest forever after the order of Melchizedek." Hebrews 8:1. Catholics find the roots of their priesthood in the tradition of Melchizedek

---

18. Genesis gives no information on the parentage of or death of Melchizedek, he is seen here as a type of Christ, representing a priesthood that is unique and eternal.

(See CCC, 1544).[19] The one priesthood of Christ: (1544) *Everything that the priesthood of the Old Covenant prefigured finds its fulfillment in Christ Jesus, the "one mediator between God and men."* The Christian tradition considers Melchizedek, "priest of God Most High," as a prefiguration of the priesthood of Christ, the unique "high priest after the order of Melchizedek"; "holy, blameless, unstained."[20]

Without father or mother, without genealogy, without beginning of days or end of life, resembling the Son of God, he remains a priest forever." Christians believe that Jesus is the Messiah spoken of as "a priest forever in the order of Melchizedek" (Ps. 110:4), and so Jesus plays the role of the king-priest once and for all. According to the writer of Hebrews (7:13-17), Jesus is considered a priest in the order of Melchizedek because, like Melchizedek, Jesus was not a descendant of Aaron, and thus would not qualify for the Jewish priesthood under the Law of Moses.

---

19. Catechism of the Catholic Church July 22, 2016. "The Christian tradition considers Melchizedek, "priest of God Most High," as a prefiguration of the priesthood of Christ, the unique "high priest after the order of Melchizedek;" 16 "holy, blameless, unstained," See also the Roman Pontifical ordination of Priest 22, Prayer of Consecration.
20. See Hebrews 7.

CHAPTER 4

Her Royal Banquet

Pettersburg speaks of a Royal Banner and the Royal Banquet Chamber. The most famous of all banqueting houses exists in England and is known as *The Banqueting House, Whitehall*. This structure stands as the best-known survivor of the architectural genre of banqueting houses and the only remaining component of the Palace of Whitehall. The structure itself was intended for royal receptions, ceremonies and masquerade performances. Pettersburg would have been familiar with the Royal Households of the United Kingdom. These households are the collective departments that support members of the British Royal Family. They vary considerably in size, from the large Royal Household that supports the Sovereign to the household of the Duke and Duchess of Cambridge and the Prince, with fewer than ten members. The lesser households are funded from the Civil List annuities, paid to their respective royal employers for their public duties, and all reimbursed to HM Treasury by the Queen.

In addition to the royal officials and support staff, the Sovereign's household incorporates representatives of other estates of the Realm, including the Government, the Military, and the Church. Government whips, defense chiefs, several clerics, scientists, musicians, poets, and artists hold honorary positions within the Royal Household. In this way, the Royal Household may be seen as having a symbolic, as well as a practical, function: exemplifying the Monarchy's close relationship with other parts of the Constitution and national life.

Royal Notice

Again we encounter Pettersburg invoking the name priesthood of Melchizedek. It would seem logical that Pettersburg would be asserting priestly superiority over governmental (Ministers) authority, given the nature of ministerial control by colonial authorities and those ministers that replaced European rule after African and Caribbean independence. We can deduce from scripture what Pettersburg was proclaiming by invoking the Royal Notice. According to scholars, the Royal Order of Melchizedek has two offices or ordained authorities of operation on earth. These are two interdependent entities: the *kingdom* and *priesthood*. Both of these interdependent authorities were intended to work in harmony and unity and to be mutually supportive.

Aaron is rebuked and Mechizedek is raised. According to the Book of Exodus, Aaron first functioned as Moses' assistant. Because Moses complained that he could not speak well, God appointed Aaron as Moses' "prophet" Moses said to the Lord:

> *"Pardon your servant, Lord. I have never been eloquent, neither in the past nor since you have spoken to your servant. I am slow of speech and tongue." The Lord said to him, "Who gave human beings their mouths? Who makes them deaf or mute? Who gives them sight or makes them blind? Is it not I, the Lord? Now go; I will help you speak and will teach you what to say." But Moses said, "Pardon your servant, Lord. Please send someone else." Then the Lord's anger burned against Moses and he said, "What about your brother, Aaron the Levite? I know he can speak well. He is already on his way to meet you, and he will be glad to see you. You shall speak to him and put words in his mouth; I will help both of you speak and will teach you what to do. He will speak to the people for you, and it will be as if he were your mouth and as if you were God to him. But take this staff in your hand so you can perform the signs with it."* (Exodus 4:10-17) Then the Lord said to Moses, *"See, I have made you like God to Pharaoh, and your brother Aaron will be your prophet."* (Exodus 7:1)

Pettersburg is separating Revivalists with common people, particularly those that are non-believers. The Revivalists according the Pettersburg have been waiting for the Kingdom of Ethiopia as Christians wait for the resurrection of and return of Christ to his Kingdom.

CHAPTER 5
The Book's Compound Limped Cover

Pettersburg re-emphasized the idea of Black Supremacy. This is not meant to stress a devaluing of non-Black life but to stress the aspirations of a people that had come out of slavery, colonialism and segregation. Black Supremacy finds its greatest support as a major tenant of Rastafari, in that Rastafari is for and by Black people. This is not an overtly militant stance but one that stresses the connectedness of Black people throughout the Diaspora.

CHAPTER 6
Obeah

Obeah (sometimes spelled Obi, Obea, or Obia) is a term used by the Igbo tribe of Nigeria, and also in the West Indies to refer to religious practices developed among West African slaves, specifically of Igbo origin. Some modern historians have argued Obeah originated from the Ashanti and Koromantin tribes of Africa on the Gold Coast, and that imported slaves introduced it to the Caribbean as early as the mid 17th century.

Obeah has been referred to and is similar to other Afro-American religions including Palo, Vodou, Santería, and Hoodoo. Obeah is practiced in Haiti, the Bahamas, Barbados, Belize, Dominica, Guyana, Suriname, Trinidad and Tobago and other Caribbean nations. Obeah men were treated with the utmost respect and fear by all who met him. The Obeah man and women played a prominent role in the Caribbean slave societies from the beginning of the Transatlantic Slave Trade. They functioned as community leaders and teachers of the African folk's cultural heritage. Many Africans believed that the Obeah man had within his power the ability to make people invincible, resuscitate the dead, cure diseases, protect a man from the consequences of his crimes. The Obeah man's most powerful gift was not his ability to steal people's shadows, as the act of obeah or "hexing" was described, but his intricate knowledge of herbs and poisons.

African slaves usually practiced Obeah for self-interested, instrumental purposes; this faith also aided them as a source of strength and resistance against slavery. The practice of Obeah is the belief that one can use certain spirits or supernatural forces to work with or against the living. In order to marginalize and destroy Obeah the British used the term Obeah to describe all slave acts and practices that were considered supernatural or evil, such as rituals and fetishes. This move by the British was intended to marginalize and stigmatize this religious practice among Black people who were introduced to Christianity through slavery.

What is most important for Pettersburg is the idea that many Obeah of the Caribbean were thought to have knowledge of medicine and many believed that Obeah "poisoned" their enemies. In the Caribbean plantations, this being the preferred and most effective tool that this practitioner of "magic" had at his disposal. Through the use of herbs and medicine, the Obeah man, was able to "miraculously" cure or poison (Obeah) a person to death. Because White or European colonial medicine was seen as barbaric, particularly the practice of bloodletting many Africans sought Obeah rather than be exposed to infantile medical practices of the time.

Balm Yards would be declared off limits to Obeah. Also included were Fortune Tellers, Old Hige (Old Haig in Guyana, soucouyant in Trinidad) were witches. Some scholars have argued that the old higge was rooted in African tradition described among the Nupe. Pettersburg places limits on a large number of animals, particularly reptiles and rodents as these animals have been forbidden by the Abrahamic religions. In particular, Islam strictly forbids the consumption of reptiles, such as crocodiles and snakes. Reptiles are also forbidden in Judaism. In other cultures, foods such as alligator are treasured as delicacies, and the animals are raised commercially. In most Western cultures, rats and mice are considered either unclean vermin or pets and thus unfit for human consumption, traditionally being seen as carriers of the plague.

CHAPTER 7
Ethiopia's Balmy Yard Poison No. 666

Six hundred and sixty-six is called the "number of the Beast" in chapter 13 of the Book of Revelation, of the New Testament.

> *"Then I saw a second beast, coming out of the earth. It had two horns like a lamb, but it spoke like a dragon. It exercised all the authority of the first beast on its behalf, and made the earth and its inhabitants worship the first beast, whose fatal wound had been healed. And it performed great signs, even causing fire to come down from heaven to the earth in full view of the people. Because of the signs it was given power to perform on behalf of the first beast, it deceived the inhabitants of the earth. It ordered them to set up an image in honor of the beast who was wounded by the sword and yet lived. The second beast was given power to give breath*

to the image of the first beast, so that the image could speak and cause all who refused to worship the image to be killed. It also forced all people, great and small, rich and poor, free and slave, to receive a mark on their right hands or on their foreheads, so that they could not buy or sell unless they had the mark, which is the name of the beast or the number of its name. This calls for wisdom. Let the person who has insight calculate the number of the beast, for it is the number of a man. That number is 666."

Biblical scholars have argued that John the Baptist, in his references to the "Beast" may have been referring to the Roman Empire; the seven heads represent the emperors.[21] So we can make the assumption that Pettersburg could have been referring to the British Empire and those Blacks that collaborated with the colonial oppressors.

We also know that the number six implies imperfection. Often, numbers are used as symbols in the Bible. Seven typically represents completeness or perfection. Six, being one short of seven, can denote something incomplete or flawed in God's eyes, and it can be associated with God's enemies—"In still another battle, which took place at Gath, there was a huge man with six fingers on each hand and six toes on each foot—twenty-four in all. He also was descended from Rapha." (1 Chronicles 20:6; And in Daniel 3:1): "King

---

21. There is no consensus as to the identity of the Roman emperors. The number seven (rev 17:9) suggests that all the emperors are meant.

Nebuchadnezzar made an image of gold, sixty cubits high and six cubits wide, and set it up on the plain of Dura in the province of Babylon."[22]

Pettersburg alludes to the poison given as medicine would lead to not only death but would signify the patient's cooperation with Lucifer. We are reminded of the covetous nature of humanity as Pettersburg warns us that the desire to cohabit with another's wife brings out our snake-like dispositions.

Pettersburgh uses the phrase: Bline, which in many urban areas refers to when someone takes a sexual innuendo as to make it uncomfortable for the others, and embarrassing themselves due to lack of social skills or grace.

Abortions have always been a controversial topic within the Black community, particularly among conservative religious elements and by those who fear that Planned Parenthood of America, Inc. (PPFA) was designed to destroy the Black family. Planned Parenthood, is a nonprofit organization that provides reproductive health care in the United States and globally. PPFA has its roots in Brooklyn, New York, where Margaret Sanger opened the first birth control clinic in the U.S. in 1916. Sanger founded the American Birth Control League in 1921, which changed its name to Planned Parenthood in 1942. Many have claimed that Margaret Sanger was

---

22. Giant statues were common in antiquity. A cubit was about a foot and a half. The proportions of this statute suggest a comedic strike against the King.

racist, but there have been no attributed quotes from Sanger that indicate that she harbored any racists views of African Americans. It is true that Margaret Sanger once gave a talk before a women's branch of the Ku Klux Klan in an effort to advocate controlled births but no evidence that she held any personal affinity for the racist organization.

CHAPTER 8

Perfect Baptism under Water

White supremacy has been defined, rather astutely by George Fredrickson as "attitudes ideologies and policies associated with blatant forms of White or European dominance of non-White populations." Petersburg attempts to assert the domination of Black Supremacy over White. The upending of White Supremacy by Black Supremacy should not be seen as a reversal of racist attitudes but the necessity out of the sheer will for the Black race to survive nearly 400 years of White genocide of non-White populations.

We are treated to the rise of Ethiopia, Africa and Egypt not as manifestations of European or White dominance.

Baptism is an important context that Jesus ordained Baptism: *"Therefore go and make disciples of all nations, baptizing them in the name of the Father and of the Son and the Holy Spirit, and teaching them to obey everything I have commanded you. And surely I am with you always, to the very end of the age."* (Matthew 28:19-20)

Pettersburg is urging that Black men and women to get baptized. Early Rastafari insisted that they were, in fact, Christians and Baptism was central to building a foundation to the faith. Baptism yokes Christians to Christ. In Romans 6:3-4: *"Or don't you know that all of us who were baptized into Christ Jesus were baptized into his death? We were therefore buried with him through baptism into death so that, just as Christ was raised from the dead through the glory of the Father, we too may live a new life."*[23]

---

23. Baptism is the prerequisite for entrance into the community of Jesus.

CHAPTER 9
Perfect Baptism Under Water

Before Ethiopia was visualized as the Promised Land, it too must be resurrected by its own baptism. The Equinoctial Equinox refers to the quality of night and day and to the time when the sun crosses the plane of the earth's equator, making night and day of approximately equal length all over the earth and occurring about March 21 (vernal equinox or spring equinox) and September 22 (autumnal equinox).

The term Land of Corn and wine comes from a well-known gospel hymn Beulah Land written by Edgar Page Stites (1836–1921) in either 1875 or 1876. The hymn concludes with the chorus:

> I've reached the *land of corn and wine,*
> And all it's riches freely mine;
> Here shines undimmed one blissful day,
> For all my night has passed away.
> *Chorus:*

> O Beuhla Land, sweet Beuhla Land,
> As on thy highest mount I stand,
> O look away across the sea,
> Where mansions are prepared for me,
> And view the shining glory-shore,
> My heav'n, my home for evermore!

The hymn derives from the King James Version of Isaiah 62:4; *"Thou shalt no more be termed Forsaken; neither shall thy land any more be termed Desolate; but thou shalt be called Hephzibah and thy land Beulah; for the LORD delighteth in thee, and thy land shall be married."* The verse is about the return of the Hebrew from their exile in Babylon in which the Hebrew shall no longer be called Forsaken, but Hephzibah (My Delight Is in Her), and Jerusalem shall no longer be called Desolate, but Beulah (Married). This implies the Hebrew have returned to the worship of God.

The idea the hymn presents is that Heaven can be seen from Beulah land comes from John Bunyan's Pilgrim's Progress in which he states "Therefore it is, I say, that the Enchanted ground is placed so nigh to the land Beulah and so near the end of their race [i.e., Heaven]."

The Jordan River runs through the land and history of the Bible, giving its waters a spiritual significance that sets it aside from other rivers. The Jordan is significant for Jews because the tribes of Israel under Joshua crossed the river on dry ground to enter the Promised Land after years of wandering in the desert. It is significant for Christians because John the Baptist baptized Jesus in the waters of the Jordan. The prophets Elijah and Elisha also crossed the river dry-shod; and the Syrian general Naaman was healed of leprosy after washing in the Jordan at Elisha's direction.

CHAPTER 10
Perfect Baptism Under Water

An Ethiopian Eunuch who was baptized by Phillip. The most interesting telling is Acts 8:26-40.[24] The Eunuch, a court official of Candace, queen of the Ethiopians, is seen reading Isaiah. Phillip runs to him and asks: "Do you understand what you are reading?"[25] The Eunuch, looking inquisitively replies, "How can I, unless someone guides me?" Phillip tells the Ethiopian the gospel of Jesus, and as they passed some water he shouted, "See, here is water! What prevents me from being baptized?" When the Chariot was stopped Phillip, and the Ethiopian went down to the water, and he was baptized. When they came out of the water, the Spirit of the Lord came and carried

---

24. According to sources the account of the conversion of the Ethiopian is intended to demonstrate the spread of Christianity beyond Judaism. This is in keeping with the plan of God. The story is given a supernatural feel with the introduction of angel.
25. Candace is not a proper name but the title of a Nubian Queen.

Phillip away, and the Eunuch never saw him again. The Eunuch went away rejoicing in the Lord.

CHAPTER 11

His and Her Majesty King Alpha and Queen Omega, Marriage Diploma

Pettersburg symbolizes the idea of the Black Kingdom rooted in both creation and destruction: the beginning and the end. Its triumph is Black supremacy as a counter to White supremacy.

Terrestrial Affidavit

Pettersburg testifies to the relationship between Lady Pettersburg and himself. This is a consistent theme throughout the RPS. This again recognizes the significance of Pettersburg's Queen as an integral part of his theology. This in many ways is contrary to the western notion that the female role in theology is one of negation or that has caused man to suffer his fate of damnation through temptation in the Garden of Eden.

CHAPTER 12
The Holy Ceremony of the Mortals

Continuing with the theme of Queen Lula May Fitz Balintine Pettersburg as a founder of the Ethiopian (Virgin) dynasty we see that it is through this marriage of the Alpha and Omega that unifies Black men and women through a royal lineage. This is why particularly among Rastafari that the use of the words king and queen are meant to signify the divinity of the Black man and Woman from the Royal house of Ethiopia extending back to the Solomonic dynasty.

We then see a contrast between what Pettersburg stated as "Black supremacy" and "White supremacy." Pettersburg attempts to make a distinction between the two worldviews. From the perspective of Africans brought to the Americas one can appreciate why the distinctions must be drawn. White supremacy was used to create a subordinated class of laborers among people of African descent. Black supremacy was the mythology used as a psychological shield against White racism.

Biblical Interpretation

Both Adam and Abraham, the father of Israel, is condemned no doubt due to Christianity being used a primary tool for the destruction of the Black race. For example Gen. 21:9–10, Ex. 20:10, 17, and Philem. 1:15–16. One of the most prominent verses: Ephesians 6:5-8 where Paul of Tarsus spoke: *"Slaves, obey your earthly masters with fear and trembling, in singleness of heart, as you obey Christ; not only while being watched, and in order to please them, but as slaves of Christ, doing the will of God from the heart. Render service with enthusiasm, as to the Lord and not to men and women, knowing that whatever good we do, we will receive the same again from the Lord, whether we are slaves or free."* Pro-slavery proponents and slave masters to seek a biblical justification for slavery used this and the previously mentioned verses, as a hammer of Black oppression.

In an unusual assertion, Pettersburg asserts that Adam, The Leper, and Abraham the Lunatic were Directors of the Marriage Proclamation of the Church Militant and White supremacy. At first glance, it would appear that Pettersburg was writing about Adam, the first man and Abraham the father of Israel. However, there did exist a leader of a fourteenth-century robber band, operating in the southeast of England in the 1330s and 1340s named Adam the Leper. The Leper and his gang's activities were directed against the royal court and its agents. The best documented of his crimes involved a nighttime attack against a London merchant with ties to Philippa of Hainault, Queen consort of Edward III. The Abraham-men were a class of beggars claiming to be lunatics allowed out of restraint, in the Tudor and Stuart periods in England. It is plausible to suggest that Pettersburg was, in fact, thinking about socio-economic class distinctions between the haves and have-nots, particularly when we see his last phrase "RICHER for POORER." This gives us a moment to suggest that he was thinking of beggars and robbers of the rich. Throughout the early 20th century the stark differences in wealth between Black people of the world and Whites would have illustrated the stark contrast between rich and poor.

CHAPTER 13
Ceremony of the Mortals

This chapter alludes to the marriage between the Black race and its claim to supremacy. It has been noted that in traditional English coronations the monarch was presented with and wore a coronation ring. The coronation ring was a symbol, particularly of the Tudor monarchy. This chapter also seems to show a form of marriage ritual that was to be used in marriage ceremonies of the followers of Pettersburg. We should also assume here that this is a proclamation of Black aspirations of love and unity and to bring forth children from these holy unions, "A Royal Child Christmas Gift."

CHAPTER 14
Fasting—How to Fast

In a searing critique of both Blacks and Whites, Pettersburg asserts that both races of men have been debased. Whites who are filthy for enslaving and colonizing much of the world, and for Blacks for having adopted White culture. From the mid 19th century one of the most important discussions in American and European society was whether Blacks and other non-White groups could be assimilated into White society. Whites believed that their racial culture had proven itself to be a superior culture to non-Whites. They believed that their advances in culture, technology, and religion gave them an inherent right to global supremacy. As Whites expanded their global reach the question was often asked what should be done with the lesser (conquered) peoples of the world? In the Americas, it was believed that the Indigenous populations would be vanquished because they were unassimilable. Blacks were long thought unassimilable and would be, as a race, destroyed or saved by

Whites but kept in an inferior state until they reached an equal level of culture and intelligence. "The White man's burden" was a term used by Whites to describe the work that was required of them to elevate Blacks to an appropriate level of civilization. Until that time Blacks would be relegated to the lower echelons of society.

Here again, we see the injection of ritual into the body the Church. We should assume that this ritual was meant to cleanse the Black body from its sinful corruption stemming from the adoption of White culture. Fasting was a cure that Pettersburg believed would psychologically and spiritually awaken the spirituality of the Black body. The duration of the fast was not stipulated. However, the Fasting was to take place roughly once per week. This cleansing ritual was to be done with a body of believers with an Elder leading. The ritual here stipulates that there is to be a washing of Salt and Water of the face and hands. Salt and water were known to be a restorative cleanser, particularly when digested or applied topically to wounds. A LOVE Feast was stipulated for every three or six months.

CHAPTER 15
The Egyptian Copyright Department

There is mention of several individuals: Queen Lula May Fitz Balintine Pettersburg, the Shepherd and Mrs. Habakkuk and Lady Indiana. The Shepherd probably refers to Shepherd Robert Athlyi Rogers author of the Holy Piby. The identities of Mrs. Habakkuk and Lady Indiana are unknown. We do know that Habakkuk was a prophet in the Hebrew Bible and author of the Book of Habakkuk. Habakkuk was of African descent, and Mrs. Habakkuk likely borrowed the name.

As King Alpha and Queen Omega there would have been a natural assertion of ownership of the earth and to rename its places.

CHAPTER 16
Speaking in Divers Tongue

We are reminded of the fateful moment in man's history when Adam was seduced by Eve, and the human family was banished from the Garden. Adam's actions led to an extravagantly loud outcry (blue murder) in respect to the human families metaphor for the banishment from our inner selves.

What perfect language and why the "Majesty of the Monarch of Life" has not appreciated the Militant fallen Angles [sic] is a mystery. Chapter sixteen delves deep into the mystery of how man was scattered upon the earth speaking diverse tongues. An excerpt from St. Augustine of Hippo's *City of God*[26] illustrating this moment may prove instructive:

> *But though these nations are said to have been dispersed according to their languages, yet the narrator recurs to*

---

26. *The City of God Against the Pagans,* often simply called The City of God, is a Christian philosophy written in Latin by Augustine of Hippo in the 5th century AD.

that time when all had but one language and explains how it came to pass that a diversity of languages was introduced. "The whole earth," he says, "was of one lip, and all had one speech. And it came to pass, as they journeyed from the east, that they found a plain in the land of Shinar, and dwelt there. And they said one to another, Come, and let us make bricks, and burn them thoroughly. And they had bricks for stone, and slime for mortar. And they said, Come, and let us build for ourselves a city and a tower whose top shall reach the sky; and let us make us a name before we be scattered abroad on the face of all the earth. And the Lord came down to see the city and the tower, which the children of men builded. And the Lord God said, Behold, the people is one, and they have all one language; and this they begin to do: and now nothing will be restrained from them, which they have imagined to do. Come, and let us go down, and confound there their language, that they may not understand one another's speech. And God scattered them thence on the face of all the earth: and they left off to build the city and the tower. Therefore the name of it is called Confusion; because the Lord did there confound the language of all the earth: and the Lord God scattered them thence on the face of all the earth."

The City of God Against the Pagans was written in response to allegations that Christianity brought about the decline of Rome and is considered one of Augustine's most influential works. The City of God is a cornerstone of Western thought, expounding on many profound questions of theology, such as the existence of evil, suffering of the righteous, the conflict between free will and divine omniscience, and the doctrine of original sin.

A supreme Monarch is given ultimate power of omniscience when the cosmic realm is referred "Heaven is no GUESSOR, long before this World was, Heaven has BEEN running co-trillions of CENTURIES ago." The suggestion seems to allude to that the language of God has been lost and therefore we have way of communicating with God. Chapter Seventeen references R.A. Rogers and the religious House of Athlyi.

CHAPTER 17

Speaking in Tongues

Traditionally there are five places in the New Testament where speaking in tongues occurs:

Mark 16:17, *"And these signs will accompany those who believe: In my name they will drive out demons; they will speak in new tongues."*

Acts 2: 1-4, *"When the day of Pentecost came, they were all together in one place. Suddenly a sound like the blowing of a violent wind came from heaven and filled the whole house where they were sitting. They saw what seemed to be tongues of fire that separated and came to rest on each of them. All of them were filled with the Holy Spirit and began to speak in other tongues as the Spirit enabled them."*

Acts 10:46, *"For they heard them speaking in tongues and praising God."*

Acts 19:6, *"When Paul placed his hands on them, the Holy Spirit came on them, and they spoke in tongues and prophesied."*

1 Cor 13:1, *"If I speak with the tongues of men and of angels, but do not have love, I have become a noisy gong or a clanging cymbal."*

This means of communication has been an accepted occurrence among Black Christians throughout the Diaspora. Robert Athlyi Rogers was known to be a speaker of tongues and in direct communication with an Angel named Douglass. In the Second Book of Athlyi Called Aggregation, Chapter 1, Heaven Grieved Rogers introduces us to Douglass by way of the pronouncement of an Angel in female form:

And it came to pass that the angel who had the less to say lifted her eyes to heaven and stretched forth her arms over the earth and cried, blessed be though Ethiopia, glory be the Father, though Elijah, Hosanna, Hosanna to Jehovah, praise ye Douglass the convention have triumph.

We have no idea of knowing what relationship Judge Rutherford and Pettersburg had at the time of his writing, but it appears that there might have been an adversarial relationship between the parties. Pettersburg gives acknowledgment to Marcus Garvey's "Big Universal Name is The Universal Negro Improvement Association and African Communities League." Garvey is referred to as the "pilot." This term (along with Shepard) was used by Rogers in the Piby to describe his mission to lead his people:

The Lord spake saying, "I will march with the Athlyians, I will pilot them, and stear them. I will recharge them and I, through their Shepherd, shall command them. Verily, there shall be no halting until they have conquered the Devil, banished His Hell and reconstruct the earth upon righteous and clean principles."

CHAPTER 18
My Rain Bow Circle Throne

Traditionally the Rainbow Circle Throne has been referred to, particularly by the Niyabinghi Order as a permanent seat of the ever-living Almighty, Haile Selassie I. The Rainbow Throne seat has been historically linked to the Kingdom of Abyssinia a direct inheritance from Emperor Menelik I, son of King Solomon and Queen Makeda of Sheba. The throne is situated on Mt. Zion and is known as the Ark or Light or City of Jah. According to the Niyabinghi tradition established in Genesis 9:12-17:

> *God said, "This is the sign of the covenant that I make between me and you and every living creature that is with you, for all future generations: I have set my bow in the clouds, and it shall be a sign of the covenant between me and the earth. When I bring clouds over the earth and the bow is seen in the clouds, I will remember my covenant that is between me and you and every living creature of all flesh; and the waters shall never again*

become a flood to destroy all flesh. When the bow is in the clouds, I will see it and remember the everlasting covenant between God and every living creature of all flesh that is on the earth." God said to Noah, "This is the sign of the covenant that I have established between me and all flesh that is on the earth."

Revelation 4:3

And the one seated there looks like jasper and carnelian, and around the throne is a rainbow that looks like an emerald.

Revelation 21:10-24

And in the spirit[a] he carried me away to a great, high mountain and showed me the holy city Jerusalem coming down out of heaven from God. It has the glory of God and a radiance like a very rare jewel, like jasper, clear as crystal. It has a great, high wall with twelve gates, and at the gates twelve angels, and on the gates are inscribed the names of the twelve tribes of the Israelites; on the east three gates, on the north three gates, on the south three gates, and on the west three gates. And the wall of the city has twelve foundations, and on them are the twelve names of the twelve apostles of the Lamb. The angel[b] who talked to me had a measuring rod of gold to measure the city and its gates and walls. The city lies foursquare, its length the same as its width; and he measured the city with his rod, fifteen hundred miles;[c] its length and width and height are equal.

He also measured its wall, one hundred forty-four cubits[d] by human measurement, which the angel was using. The wall is built of jasper, while the city is pure gold, clear as glass. The foundations of the wall of the city are adorned with every jewel; the first was jasper, the second sapphire, the third agate, the fourth emerald, the fifth onyx, the sixth carnelian, the seventh chrysolite, the eighth beryl, the ninth topaz, the tenth chrysoprase, the eleventh jacinth, the twelfth amethyst. And the twelve gates are twelve pearls, each of the gates is a single pearl, and the street of the city is pure gold, transparent as glass.

I saw no temple in the city, for its temple is the Lord God the Almighty and the Lamb. And the city has no need of sun or moon to shine on it, for the glory of God is its light, and its lamp is the Lamb. The nations will walk by its light, and the kings of the earth will bring their glory into it.

CHAPTER 19
Ethiopia's Triumphant Proclamation

An appeal to Black people to shed their given nationalities, particularly those living in Jamaica. Pettersburg noted that in formerly colonized countries (As well as the United States) Blacks are deceived into believing that the Masters had their best interest at heart.

Pettersburg pronounces his demand that all natural forces of fire, brimstone, "vulcannon," thunder and lightening belongs to him. He speaks with supreme authority and those under the sound of his voice will and must obey. This is a severe pronouncement, but it alludes to the need for complete loyalty as it relates to the message to the Black man and woman. Heading this message will lead to salvation and redemption of Black people when they come to an understanding that they are deceived in the land of their oppression.

CHAPTER 20

The Royal Swaddling of Jesus and John the Baptist

A girdle or belt worn about the head and loins by John the Baptist and Jesus Christ is indicative of the theological connection between Black people and divinity. This pronouncement is one of the unique places in the RPS where we see sacred clothing being worn reminiscent of the Gartel or Tzitzis worn by Orthodox Jews. The Monarch's girdle is described and instructions on how to be worn. This simple action would work to develop an inner spirituality with a physical act of wearing the garments.

Pettersburg expresses the divine nature of the trinity as a Tri-Divinity. This divinity is expressed in his being, Queen Lula and Jesus.

CHAPTER 21

The Load-Stone Lepor

This chapter speaks of The Balm Yard No. 666. Revelations 13:16-18:

> Also it causes all, both small and great, both rich and poor, both free and slave, to be marked on the right hand or the forehead, so that no one can buy or sell who does not have the mark, that is, the name of the beast or the number of its name.[18] This calls for wisdom: let anyone with understanding calculate the number of the beast, for it is the number of a person. Its number is six hundred sixty-six.[27]

Again we see references to the Balm Yard, a place of healing often doctored by an Obeah. The magic of the Obeah was often seen as an anathema to many who were Christianized including Pettersburg.

---

27. Other authorities read this as six-hundred sixteen.

CHAPTER 22
The Law of Resurrection

A reminder of the laws that govern justice. Black people will come to Honor, and the other race will come to dishonor. But before this prophecy can be fulfilled every Black man and woman must make the crooked road straight.

There can be no rebuilding of the Temple of Solomon. Black people will need a much larger vessel to house the new Black Kingdom. Pettersburg fashions himself as the master builder.

CHAPTER 23

Ethiopia's Banqueting Chamber

A royal feast where merriment and love of the virgin princess are to be had. This is a consummation of the ceremonial meal uniting Black men and women. It is necessary for Blacks united to gather to celebrate their unity by feasting. In previous chapters, Pettersburg set out the parameters for feast days. Here Pettersburg specifies a liturgical calendar: Birth, Death, Marriage, Home, Friends, Assembly, Rest, Christmas, and Business transactions.

CHAPTER 24
Government

The RPS was a forward-thinking text, yet at the same time, the RPS calls for a prohibition on miscegenation in a seemingly retrograde pronouncement. Historically, "race mixing" between Black and White people was taboo in the United States until Loving v. Virginia (1967). So-called anti-miscegenation laws, barring Blacks and Whites from marrying or having sex, were established in colonial America.

The historical taboo among American Whites surrounding White-Black relationships can be seen as a historical consequence of the oppression and racial segregation of African-Americans. In many U.S. states, interracial marriage was already illegal when the term miscegenation was invented in 1863. The first laws banning interracial marriage were introduced in the late 17th century in the slave-holding colonies of Virginia (1691) and Maryland (1692). Later these laws also spread to colonies and states where slavery did not exist. Miscegenation was never declared illegal in the British

West Indies, and the populations of Guyana, Belize, Jamaica, and Trinidad are among the worlds most diverse populations. RPS calls for stable marriages and places a prohibition on marrying those that are divorced.

Education had always been seen as a benchmark of progress for Black people. Denied a basic education throughout slavery Blacks desired to educate both themselves and their posterity. RPS calls for compulsory education so that the faithful would be seen as "respectful diplomats" that can reply satisfactorily to everyone that approaches or writes on any subject. However, Pettersburg states "Do not try to let your Wife, or Husband, or Family feel small because you got more College filth in your HEAD." Pettersburg warns that the Black college educated must be wary of corruption and to remain loyal to family and the Black race.

CHAPTER 25

The Owner of the Most Holy Theocracy, K.A.Q.O.

A simple pronouncement of a theocratic system of government in which priests rule in the name of God. Pettersburg and his Queen Lula May Balintine Pettersburg.

CHAPTER 26
World's Building

It is unclear how the RPS intends to use communication for the propagation of Pettersburg's kingdom. But certainly, the idea here would be to spread the message of the RPS throughout the Black Diaspora. The birth of the monarch is seen here as Queen Lula's first born. By the 1920s New York City was close to being seen as the world's capital. But it is uncertain if the Pettersburg's were married in the City. Again we see Pettersburg declaring both himself and Queen Lula as the beginning and the end, Alpha and Omega.

CHAPTER 27
World's Building

Cognizant of the fact that the passing of generational wealth is partly responsible for the ascension of the White race, the RPS desires that Blacks work toward the same: "And children must INHERIT their PARENTS WEALTH." It is described here that Black children are targeted for destruction because of this fact. Here we see the warning again to not marry anyone from "White supremacy." That Whites, in their hearts, will ultimately retreat to slavery. It is clear where Pettersburg stands on his relationship with Whites. We have to understand the racial climate of the period, particularly that of the United States. For example, in a demonstration of White power and supremacy on August 8, 1925, thirty thousand Ku Klux Klan members marched in White hooded regalia through the streets of Washington, D.C., America's capital. The Washington Post noted that the KKK, as they are often called, were given a friendly reception in all corners of the United States. The KKK is a White terrorist organization that murdered thousands of people of African descent gruesomely. These murders were intended to remind Blacks and other non-Whites that America was and is a White nation.

CHAPTER 28
General Marcus Garvey and Bishops Rogers

A reminder that Garvey stood for the repatriation of Blacks to Africa. R.A. Roger's The Holy Piby is mentioned and again shows the relationship between the three men (Howell, Rogers and Pettersburg) and their attempt to re-align Black religious consciousness. John Wilson Bell appears to be the master of ceremony in Pettersburg's ordination in 1924. Apostolic succession does not appear to have been something necessary, but without more information, we are left to speculate whether Pettersburg, through irony, is condemning or praising Bell.

CHAPTER 29

The Eternal Law Office

There appears to be a connection between false prophets and minsters and those in the business and legal profession. We have already seen that Pettersburg had a deep suspicion of college educated and those that were seen to have some power within society. (A direct contradiction to the belief of creating an educated society of Black men and women) Here he reminds the faithful that the "lepors,"[sic] ministers and lawyers are one in the same. A reference to Matthew 25:10 suggests that those that follow the false teaching of Adam-Abraham-Angle-Saxon will be shut out from the banquet room: *And while they went to buy it, the bridegroom came, and those who were ready went with him into the wedding banquet; and the door was shut.*

CHAPTER 30

The Soldiers at Camp and the Police Dept.

The legal system throughout the western hemisphere has always been corrupted to deny Blacks justice. Police Departments have been notoriously brutal in using violence to suppress Black rights. Anyone, according to the RPS that follows the teachings of Christianity is at odds with the resurrection and redemption of Black Supremacy.

CHAPTER 31
Black Supremacy's Infant's Diploma

It appears that the RPS provides a template for the information that should be collected at the time of the infant births or their graduation into the Church.

CHAPTER 32
His and Her Monarch the African Potentate

A firm stand is taken here on the blood shed by Blacks to redeem the White church. Petersburg witnessed the onslaught of European colonialism that came to be indicative of late 19th and early 20th centuries. We see the link here with the name Ciaphas as a means to interject the idea of a conspiracy to destroy the Black biblical and cultural history. Joseph Caiaphas, in the New Testament, was the Jewish high priest who is said to have organized the plot to kill Jesus. One of the most notable themes in the RPS is the takeover and corruption of the Body of Christ and the Bible. The RPS maintains that the history as witnessed in the Bible is a Black history given up and reconstituted for the propagation of the control of Black bodies through White supremacy. The constant process of giving of that which is sacred and then the giving of Black bodies in slavery to enrich White supremacy is clearly noted.

CHAPTER 33

Ethiopia's School, College & University

Revelation 22:12-13: *See, I am coming soon; my reward is with me, to repay according to everyone's work. I am the Alpha and the Omega, the first and the last, the beginning and the end.* Mention of the tree of life here alludes to the River of Life where an angel appears and show the river of the water of life. One either side of the river was the tree of life, with twelve kinds of fruit and leaves for the healing of the nations. A place where there is no night, no sun as God's light will illuminate, and they will reign forever. The RPS ties the reign of King Alpha and Queen Omega to Revelations' prophecy of the second coming of Christ. While the suggestion has been made earlier that Petersburg pronounced a deep suspicion of the college-educated we see here that schools, colleges, and universities can be used to further the aims of the King Alpha and Queen Omega.

CHAPTER 34

Black Supremacy's Patten Officer

Suspicion of government, professions and educated are the themes of this chapter. Most likely the professional classes were increasingly coming to dominate life in the British West Indies as well as in the United States. The suspicion of professionals is not without merit. The professional and educated classes of the British West Indies were used as proxies by Europeans to control the Black masses and peasantry. This was a well-known tactic used by the Europeans to control Black colonies. Control of Black populations would not have been nearly as effective had there not been a middle class of British educated and controlled Black classes. The educated were held up as models for the Black peasantry to emulate. The Black middle class were middle managers used to place a layer of control between Whites and the Black masses. Further, Whites were used as models for the Black middle class to emulate, thereby creating a system of rewards and punishments for the rewards of middle class life.

CHAPTER 35
Eve, the Mother of Evil

This chapter reasserts the claim of Black Supremacy in a way that insists upon the rightful heir to the throne of David, and therefore Black roots are the "Creators of Creation." References here are to the Tree of Knowledge in the Garden of Eden. Eve again does not fair well here. She is called the Mother of Evil for having led Adam to eat of the Tree and to be banished from the Garden. The story of the fall and subsequent use of Biblical text to justify slavery and the continued oppression of Black people through colonialism justifies the derision of Adam, Abraham and the Anglo-Saxon. Further, the idea of an Anglo-Saxon Jesus defies logic and therefore would have been and still is seen as a shallow but effective means of White washing the Bible. References are made to Genesis Chapter 2 as the story of Creation. A contradictory story of Creation was given in Chapter 1.

CHAPTER 36
The Eternal Come Back

For the first time, we are given an indication of the name "Bulah" as applied to Queen Omega. This could either signal a name used throughout her life or a reference to Beulah the feminine name originally a Hebrew word used in the book of Isaiah as a prophesied treatment of the land of Israel. In the King James version of the Bible, the word literally means married.

Continued references to Pay Master and Balance sheet probably suggest that there will be some reward and account for the deeds done here on earth by the righteous and the unjust, as both will ultimately have to meet the Pay Master and each balance sheet will be reviewed under the weight of one's life.

CHAPTER 37
None Matrimonial Prosecution

There is no doubt that there was a deep mistrust of post-colonial governments in the British West Indies during the early 20th century. These holdover governments still in existence at the end of the First World War were still determining outcomes.

CHAPTER 38

His and Her Majesty King Melchiszedek's Affidavit

Melchizedek is the king of Salem and priest of El Elyon ("God most high") mentioned in the 14th chapter of the Book of Genesis. He brings out bread and wine and blesses Abram and El Elyon. In Christianity, according to the Epistle to the Hebrews, Jesus Christ is identified as "a priest forever in the order of Melchizedek", and so Jesus assumes the role of High Priest once and for all.

Genesis Chapter 14:17:

After his return from the defeat of Chedorlaomer and the kings who were with him, the king of Sodom went out to meet him at the Valley of Shaveh. And King Melchizedek of Salem brought out bread and wine; he was priest of God Most High. He blessed him and said "Blessed be Abram by God Most High,[d]maker of heaven and earth; and blessed be God Most High,who has delivered your enemies into your hand!"

People of African descent used the story of the Exodus as a mirror for divine intervention in their plight from bondage used the story of the Exodus. As the Hebrews were led out of Egypt so too were Blacks led from bondage at various times and places throughout the Americas.

We again see various themes here of Pettersburg as the "Paymaster," "King Alpha."

In the Rabbinic tradition of the Talmud, the Obadiah is said to have been a convert to Judaism from Edom, a descendant of Eliphaz, the friend of Job. He is identified with the Obadiah who was the servant of Ahab, and it is said that he was chosen to prophesy against Edom because he was himself an Edomite. Obadiah received the gift of prophecy for having hidden the "hundred prophets" (1 Kings 18:4) from the persecution of Jezebel. He hid the prophets in two caves so that if those in one cave should be discovered those in the other might yet escape (1 Kings 18:3-4).

Obadiah was very rich, but all his wealth was expended in feeding the poor prophets, until, in order to be able to continue to support them, finally he had to borrow money at interest from Ahab's son Jehoram. Obadiah's fear of God was one degree higher than that of Abraham; and if the house of Ahab had been capable of being blessed, it would have been blessed for Obadiah's sake.

The Book of Obadiah concerns the judgment of Edom and the restoration of Israel. The book consists of a single chapter, divided into twentyone verses, making it the shortest book in the Hebrew Bible. In Judaism and Christianity, its authorship is attributed to a prophet who lived in the Assyrian Period and named himself in the first verse, Obadiah. His name means "servant of Yahweh". In Christianity, the Book of Obadiah is a minor prophet of the Old Testament. In Judaism, Obadiah is considered a "later prophet," placed in the last section (Nevi'im of the Tanakh), where it is one of the "Twelve Prophets."

CHAPTER 39

New Testament Port

We see a shift here from the Old Testament to the New Testament, something that has not resonated throughout many of the proto-Rastafari biblical texts. Proto-Rastafari texts have been primarily concerned with re-establishing their links back to the House of David and the reclaiming Black people as the rightful chosen people. There is a direct challenge to the Anglo Saxon interpretation the Anglo-Saxon version of the creation.

We see a return to Revelation 22 and the Tree of Life. In Revelation 12-13 the vision of a woman clothed with the sun and the great red dragon, with seven heads and tens horns and the seven diadems on his head is referenced here. Michael and his Angels defeat the Red Dragon and his Angels. Defeated the devil and his Angels are then thrown to earth. With this defeat, God asserts her dominion over the heavens and the earth. So too has Pettersburg asserted that "I am your Eternal Pay Master on the Train of Holy Time YOUR JOINT AIR and Keeper of The Tree of Life, Your FRIEND."

CHAPTER 40

The Ethiopian People's Ordination

Ethiopia stands as the People of God. People of Ethiopia are Black men and women chosen by God to lead the Triumphant Dynasty. A clear demarcation is made between the Abrahamic family and the Ethiopian family. Pettersburg reminds of his earlier proclamation that made it clear to marry Whites will lead to the destruction of the Black family. This has to be seen in context to the complete prohibition of inter-racial marriages, particularly in the United States until Supreme Court decision of Loving v. Virginia (1967) outlawed the prohibition of inter-racial marriage.

References are made to the name "Antediluvia." Antediluvian means "before the deluge." It is the time referred to in the Bible between the fall of humans and the Genesis Flood (Noachian Deluge) in the bible. The narrative takes up chapters 1–6 (excluding the flood narrative) of the Book of Genesis. The term found its way into early geology until the late Victorian era. We have an imagery of Black people in central roles in the bible. Here, King Noah, a Black man is drowned because of the original sin of Adam.

CHAPTER 41

No. 1 The Bible Editor

David is put with the Chaff: "The wicked are not so, but are like chaff that the wind drives away"(Psalm 1:4). Pettersburg calls out his Brother Prince Emanuel. This should not be confused with Prince Emanuel Charles Edwards (1915–1994), who was a Jamaican Rastafari who founded the Bobo Shanti order in 1958 in Bull Bay in Jamaica. At the time of this publishing, Emanuel Charles Edwards would have been a minor child. Given the RPS's tenor Psalm 2 is an appropriate statement of God's Promise to those that are chosen to carry her message. A review of Psalm 2 is appropriate here:

> Why do the nations conspire,
> and the peoples plot in vain?
> 2 The kings of the earth set themselves,
> and the rulers take counsel together,
> against the Lord and his anointed, saying,
> 3 "Let us burst their bonds asunder,

and cast their cords from us."
4 He who sits in the heavens laughs;
the Lord has them in derision.
5 Then he will speak to them in his wrath,
and terrify them in his fury, saying,
6 "I have set my king on Zion, my holy hill."
7 I will tell of the decree of the Lord:
He said to me, "You are my son;
today I have begotten you.
8 Ask of me, and I will make the nations your heritage,
and the ends of the earth your possession.
9 You shall break them with a rod of iron,
and dash them in pieces like a potter's vessel."
10 Now therefore, O kings, be wise;
be warned, O rulers of the earth.
11 Serve the Lord with fear,
with trembling 12 kiss his feet, [a]
or he will be angry, and you will perish in the way;
for his wrath is quickly kindled.
Happy are all who take refuge in him.

CHAPTER 42
The Head Biblical Interpreter of Creation

Mentioned here was the White terrorist organization the Ku Klux Klan also known as the KKK. Veterans of the Southern Confederate Army had originally founded the KKK in 1865 in Pulaski, Tennessee. One of the most famous of these early founders was Nathan Bedford Forrest (1821 – 1877) a former lieutenant general in the Confederate Army during the American Civil War. Forrest served as the first Grand Wizard of the Ku Klux Klan. Klan groups spread throughout the South as a domestic terrorist organization during the period when the U.S. government attempted to reconstruct the nation after the Civil War. During the period known as *Reconstruction* (1865-1877) the Klan increasingly targeted Blacks attempting to exercise their newly won freedom and any Whites that attempted to help them exercise their Constitutional rights. Lynchings were

Biblical Interpretation

the preferred method used by the KKK to strike fear and dread among the Black population. The National Association for the Advancement of Colored People affirmed "From 1882-1968, 4,743 lynchings occurred in the United States. Of these people that were lynched 3,446 were Black. The Blacks lynched accounted for 72.7% of the people lynched. These numbers seem large, but it is known that not all of the lynchings were ever recorded. Out of the 4,743 people lynched only 1,297 White people were lynched. That is only 27.3%. Many of the Whites lynched were lynched for helping the Black or being anti-lynching and even for domestic crimes."[28]

We see grave concern for miscegenation. This belief was rife not only in South Africa but in particular the United States. Fear that a mulatto race of people would destroy both the Black and White race consumed both Black and White racial ideology. With Blacks, the fear rested from a sense of ultimate destruction, and with Whites, it stemmed from a loss of power and control of Black people. Because of the One Drop Rule, the stated firmly that one-drop of Black blood tainted you so that you were then considered Black struck fear in White America. The fear was over the thought of a mongrelized race of people that would destroy their way of life. Pettersburg calls out what he believes is the growing sentiment of Black men consorting with White women. By the time of the publishing of the RPS one of

---

28. http://www.naacp.org/history-of-lynchings

the most celebrated figures in sports, heavyweight-boxing champion Jack Johnson had been arrested and convicted for his relationship with White women. On October 18, 1912, Johnson was arrested because his relationship with Lucille Cameron violated the Mann Act against "transporting women across state lines for immoral purposes" due to her being an alleged prostitute and due to Johnson being Black. At the time this was the most sensational story of miscegenation in the United States until Loving.

CHAPTER 43
The Man Before Adam Was

This is an assertion of Black people as the progenitors of humanity. One area to note that is that the creation of Adam is not, according to Pettersburg the beginning of mankind. The beginning of mankind is the beginning of the Black race. We are reminded again that Adam, Eve, and Abraham (as well as the Anglo-Saxon) are adversaries and are in no way part of the Black Nation. This Black Nation is the first and the last, the alpha and omega.

CHAPTER 44
My Royal Mother

Throughout the RPS we are exposed to a variety of people each in some way has helped to shape the life of Pettersburg. Pettersburg states that his virgin mother is Mrs. Ellen (Park) Johnson of Pettersburg. If this is Pettersburg birth mother is only conjecture. A search in the early 20th-century birth records might reveal Pettersburg's family relations.

CHAPTER 45
The Founder's Support Funds

It is hard to conclude what Pettersburg was attempting to do in this chapter. The acronyms have not been deciphered as no text has emerged that would provide a cipher. But if we look closely we do see acronyms that stand out. For instance Ph.D., LLD most likely stands for a doctorate of philosophy and doctor of laws respectively. We also get a sense that this is a form of justification and appeal for monetary support from the lay membership.

CHAPTER 46
Registered Library

This appears to justify the creation and maintenance of a library or sacred book repository. The collection and maintenance of Black history became a central concern of Black intellectuals such as Carter G. Woodson. Woodson (1875-1950) was an African-American historian, author, journalist and the founder of the Association for the Study of African American Life and History. A founder of The Journal of Negro History in 1915, Woodson has been cited as the "father of Black history." Because of the period that the RPS was written Pettersburg knew of the work of Woodson, but this is only conjecture. In February 1926 Woodson launched the celebration of "Negro History Week, "the precursor of Black History Month.

CHAPTER 47
The African Question

Pettersburg uses the African continent as a metaphor for Black women. Rich and fertile, she has been, as Pettersburg has asserted throughout the RPS, "raped." This debasement of female Black bodies had enriched Whites but destroyed the Black nation. Because of the vile brutality of slavery, we can assume that no earthly cures to wellness exist. During the "Scramble for Africa" in the late nineteenth century, Western European powers divided Africa and its resources into colonies at the Berlin Conference of 1884-85. By 1905, control of almost all African soil was claimed by Western European governments, with the only exceptions being Liberia, settled by African-American former slaves and Ethiopia which had successfully resisted colonization by Italy. Great Britain, France, Germany, Spain, Italy, Belgium, and Portugal all had colonies. As a result, a majority of Africa lost control of natural resources. Black people in the Americas were keenly aware that the First World War was largely fought over the control of African resources. The decolonization of Africa, particularly West Africa, began with the liberation of Ghana in 1957.

CHAPTER 47A
Atlas Survayor [sic]

The RPS consists of fifty chapters. We are alerted here the Pettersburg had intended to include twenty more chapters. We are told that problems with printing are responsible for delays in developing the fullest version of the RPS. It appears that Pettersburgh had created an additional bible that contained seventy-six chapters, but this document had been willfully destroyed by a man he called Alexander Habkkuk Coombs and his wife. Without sufficient evidence don't know if the RPS was a replacement of this seventy-six chapter bible or an addition to it.

CHAPTER 48
The Map-Making and Bible Atlas Survayor [sic]

Again a repetition of the destruction of Pettersburg's earlier biblical work as noted in Chapter 47a.

CHAPTER 48A
Owner of the Zodiac

Astrology has always held both a deep fascination by its followers and derision by its critics. Some see it as a form of pagan witchcraft and others as a spiritual art that provides insight into one's life. Pettersburg clearly denounces astrology as White supremacy and Astrologist as guilty "of the Crime of Genealogical, Sexual, Mortal Suicide."

CHAPTER 49
Psalm 50 By the Monarch Pettersburgh[29]

In a poetic play, we see Psalms being equated with being the music of the Tree of Life. Psalm 50, is indented to a psalm of instruction, according to one biblical commentary. It tells of the coming of Christ and the day of judgment, in which God will call men to account; and the Holy Ghost is the Spirit of judgment.[30] Augustine of Canterbury (born the first third of the 6th century – died probably 604) was a Catholic Benedictine monk who became the first Archbishop of Canterbury in the year 597. He is considered the "Apostle to the English" and a founder of the Catholic Church in England. A significant number of manuscripts were created under the Archbishop's tenure. Which manuscript that he is referring is unknown.

---

29. We see throughout the text the varying spelling of Pettersburg.
30. See Matthew Henry's Concise Commentary: http://www.christianity.com/bible/commentary.

CHAPTER 50
The Theological Lawgiver of Creation

A reassertion of Pettersburg's claim to the throne of the Kingdom. A pronouncement o the end of the Anglo Saxon kingdom in favor of the "powerhouse of the Great Black Supremacy, the Church triumphant. A clear assertion of the Black man as divinity and the renaming of the bible as "Holy Theocracy and Lady Diety, Creation's Supremacy." A linking of a spiritual graduation as Black people come to a self-realization of their sacred duty to awaken to their role in the Church Triumphant. Notice that this chapter is signed December 1, 1925, and the previous chapter forty-nine was signed June 2, 1926. Vulcan refers to the god of fire in ancient Roman religion and mythology. Vulcan is often depicted with a Blacksmith's hammer, and we can suppose here that Pettersburg means the theological plants (Black roots and people) must be able to face the full brunt of the Church.

At the end of the chapter, we see the diploma that is to be used for graduates. It has all of the pomp and circumstance as any educational diploma of the period. The inscription of the graduates was to include name, continent, address and business if applicable.

www.ingramcontent.com/pod-product-compliance
Lightning Source LLC
Chambersburg PA
CBHW070641160426
43194CB00009B/1540